5001276467

KT-511-736

May 1997

THE ScHARR GUIDE TO EVIDENCE-BASED PRACTICE

Andrew Booth

ScHARR

(School of Health and Related Research)

University of Sheffield

ScHARR Occasional Paper No. 97/2

Published by ScHARR (School of Health and Related Research), University of Sheffield

---

For further copies :

Suzy Paisley
Senior Information Officer
School of Health and Related Research (ScHARR)
University of Sheffield
Regent Court
30 Regent Street
Sheffield
S1 4DA

Tel: (0114) 222 5420
Fax: (0114) 272 4095
Email: scharrlib@sheffield.ac.uk

Price : £10.00 per copy (inc. p & p)
By cheque payable to : University of Sheffield

School of Health and Related Research

AN INTRODUCTION TO ScHARR

ScHARR, The School of Health and Related Research, is a large, multidisciplinary research centre located near the centre of Sheffield. It forms the northern arm of the Trent Institute for Health Services Research which also includes centres at Nottingham and Leicester Universities. The staff at the School are drawn from a wide range of disciplines and backgrounds, embracing epidemiology, health economics, management sciences, medical sociology, medical statistics, nursing research, operational research, primary care, psychology, information science and public health medicine. This broad base of skills, together with the School's close ties with local NHS Trusts and Health Authorities, makes it uniquely placed to conduct applied and methodological Health Services Research to the highest quality.

AIMS OF ScHARR

The aims of ScHARR are:

- to conduct and promote within the University, Health Services Research (HSR), judged to be excellent both nationally and internationally;

- to deliver the highest standard of teaching in HSR and related subjects,

- to provide research and consultancy services in HSR to clients outside the University, particularly to NHS Trusts and Authorities but also to other public sector bodies and private organisations;

- to be an active and vigorous member of the Trent Institute for Health Services Research.

Professor Ron Akehurst, Director

AUTHORS

Andrew Booth is Director of Information Resources in the School of Health and Related Research (ScHARR) at the University of Sheffield.

ACKNOWLEDGEMENTS

Andrew Booth would like to thank members of the **evidence-based-health** Mailbase discussion list for their valuable contributions and for their encouragement for previous versions of this Guide. He would also like to thank members of the ScHARR internal Critical Reviews Advisory Group (CRAG).

EVIDENCE-BASED PRACTICE RESOURCE GUIDE 64

Rationale for this guide

The following short guide attempts to identify some useful sources and resources in support of evidence-based practice. In most cases only materials published from 1990 onwards have been included although earlier references are easily identifiable by consulting more recent items. Exceptions are made to this five-year cut-off date where items are considered to be of particular value. The guide is divided into two main sections: the first is a bibliography of printed sources on all aspects of Evidence-based healthcare whilst the second is a resource guide of organisations, journals, databases and World Wide Web resources available to support the various stages involved in using the evidence.

What is Evidence-based Practice?

Evidence-based *medicine* (EBM) is *"the conscientious, explicit, and judicious use of current best evidence in making decisions about the care of individual patients. The practice of evidence based medicine means integrating individual clinical expertise with the best available external clinical evidence from systematic research[1]"*. Evidence-based practice is, by implication, *the systematic application of rigorous scientific methods to the evaluation of the effectiveness of health care interventions.* This can be broadened to include such considerations as appropriateness, clinical decisionmaking, economic evaluation, health technology assessment, outcomes measurement and risk management.

Although the above definition of Evidence-based Medicine from Professor David Sackett of the Centre for Evidence-based Medicine is the most familiar, many commentators prefer the definition found in a Working Paper from the Health Information Resource Unit, McMaster University, Ontario, Canada. This states that *"Evidence-based medicine (EBM) is an approach to health care that promotes the collection, interpretation, and integration of valid, important and applicable patient-reported, clinician-observed, and research-derived evidence. The best available evidence, moderated by patient circumstances and preferences, is applied to improve the quality of clinical judgments"[2].*

---

[1] Sackett DL, Rosenberg WMC , Muir Gray JA, Haynes RB and Richardson WS. Evidence based medicine : what it is and what it isn't. *British Medical Journal* 1996; 312 : 71-72.

[2] McKibbon KA, Wilczynski N, Hayward RS, Walker-Dilks CJ, Haynes RB. The medical literature as a resource for Evidence Based Care, at *http://hiru.mcmaster.ca/hiru/medline/mdl-ebc.htm*

Related Definitions

The distinction made by Sackett et al (*Clinical Epidemiology : A basic science for clinical medicine.* 2nd ed. Little, Brown & Company 1991) is as follows:-

REVIEW - *"the general term for all attempts to synthesize the results and conclusions of two or more publications on a given topic".*

OVERVIEW - *"when a review strives to comprehensively identify and track down all the literature on a topic (also called "systematic literature review")".*

META-ANALYSIS - *"when an overview incorporates a specific statistical strategy for assembling the results of several studies into a single estimate".*

The National Library of Medicine definition of **meta-analysis** states:

"A quantitative method of combining the results of independent studies (usually drawn from the published literature) and synthesizing summaries and conclusions which may be used to evaluate therapeutic effectiveness, plan new studies etc., with application chiefly in the areas of research and medicine".

Useful guides to the terminology of research studies are found in:

Haynes RB et al. More informative abstracts revisited. *Annals of Internal Medicine* 1990; 113(1) : 69-76

Goodman C. *Literature Searching and evidence interpretation for assessing health care practices.* Stockholm : SBU (Swedish Council on Technology Assessment in Health Care), 1993.

Jones R and Kinmouth AL. *Critical reading for primary care.* Oxford : Oxford University Press, 1995.

Last JM. *A Dictionary of epidemiology*, 3rd ed. Oxford : Oxford University Press, 1995.

US Congress, Office of Technology Assessment. *Identifying health technologies that work : searching for the evidence*, OTA-H-608. Appendix D - Glossary. Washington, DC : US Government Printing Office, September 1994.

The journal *Evidence Based Medicine* has started (1996; Volume 1 : Issue 2 onwards) to publish a glossary of terms used in the different types of study. The first two issues are on Therapeutics and further articles cover Diagnosis, Prognosis, Etiology, Quality Improvement and Economics.

The Centre for Evidence-based Medicine in Oxford, UK has produced a glossary of EBM terms on its World Wide Web site at:-

http://cebm.jr2.ox.ac.uk/docs/glossary.html

A clinical practice guidelines glossary containing many of the terms used by EBM and by clinical epidemiology is found on the World Wide Web at:-

http://hiru.mcmaster.ca/cpg/toolkit/glossary.htm

A glossary of EBM terms used by the Journal of Family Practice is available as:-

http://www.phymac.med.wayne.edu/jfp/glossary.htm

Andrew Booth (31/03/1997)

Bibliography of Evidence-based Practice

INTRODUCTORY MATERIAL

A useful Internet-based introduction is:- McKibbon KA, Wilczynski N, Hayward RS, Walker-Dilks CJ, Haynes RB. The medical literature as a resource for Evidence Based Care, at *http://hiru.mcmaster.ca/hiru/medline/mdl-ebc.htm* . Print based materials are as follows:-

Books

Baker M and Kirk S. *Research and development for the NHS : evidence, evaluation and effectiveness.* Oxford : Radcliffe Medical Press, 1996. [ISBN : 1-8577-5094-2]

Chalmers I and Altman DG. *Systematic reviews.* London : BMJ Publishing Group, 1995.

Crump BJ and Drummond MF *Evaluating clinical evidence : a handbook for managers.* Harlow : Longman, 1993.

Dixon R and Munro J. *Evidence based medicine : a practical workbook for clinical problem solving.* London : Butterworth-Heinemann, March 1997.

Dunn G and Everitt B. *Clinical biostatistics : an introduction to Evidence-based medicine.* London : Arnold, 1995.

Friedman LM, Furberg CD and De Mets DL. *Fundamentals of clinical trials.* 3rd ed. Mosby, 1996.

Jones R and Kinmouth AL. *Critical reading for primary care.* Oxford : Oxford University Press, 1995.

Lockett T. *Evidence-based and cost-effective medicine.* Oxford : Radcliffe Medical Press, 1997.

Miles A and Lugon M. *Effective clinical practice.* Oxford : Blackwell Science, 1996.

Muir Gray JA. *Evidence-based health care : how to make health policy and management decisions.* London : Churchill Livingstone, 1996.

Peckham M and Smith R. *Scientific basis of health services.* London : BMJ Publishing Group, 1996.

Ridsdale L. *Evidence-based general practice : a critical reader.* London : WB Saunders, 1995. [ISBN:- 0-7020-1611-X]

Sackett DL et al. *Clinical epidemiology : a basic science for clinical medicine.* 2nd ed. Little, Brown & Company : 1991.

Sackett DL et al. *Evidence-based medicine : how to practice and teach EBM.* London : Churchill Livingstone, 1996.

Reports

Appleby J, Walshe K and Ham C. *Acting on the evidence : a review of clinical effectiveness, sources of information, dissemination and implementation.* (NAHAT Research Paper 17) Birmingham : NAHAT, 1995.

Deighan M & Hitch S. (eds). *Clinical effectiveness : from guidelines to cost-effective practice.* Brentwood, Essex : Earlybrave Publications Limited, 1995.

Donald A. *Evidence-based medicine : a report from McMaster University Medical School and Teaching Hospitals : "Becoming better, faster, happier docs".* Anglia and Oxford RHA : Oxford, 1994. For further information contact 01865 226833.

Felton T and Lister G. *Consider the evidence - the NHS on the move towards evidence-based medicine.* London : Coopers and Lybrand, April 1996.

Honigsbaum F and Ham C. *Improving clinical effectiveness : the development of clinical guidelines.* Birmingham : University of Birmingham, 1996.

OMAR. *An evidence-based health care system : the case for clinical trial registries.* Bethesda, MD : National Institutes of Health. Office of Medical Applications of Research, 1993.

Sackett DL. *The Doctor's (ethical and economic) dilemma.* (OHE Annual Lecture 1996). London : Office of Health Economics, 1996. [ISBN : 0901387983].

Walshe K and Ham C. *Acting on the evidence : progress in the NHS.* Birmingham : NHS Confederation, 1997.

Journal articles, issues and book contributions

Annals of the New York Academy of Sciences 1993 December; 703 : 1-341. Special Issue on "Doing more good than harm : the evaluation of health care interventions".

Batstone G and Edwards M. Professional roles in promoting evidence-based practice. *British Journal of Health Care Management* 1996 March; 2(3) : 144-147.

Chalmers I. Assembling the evidence. In : Dunning M & Needham G (eds.). *But will it work, doctor?* Milton Keynes : Consumer Health Information Consortium, 1993.

Cohen L. McMaster's pioneer in evidence-based medicine now spreading his message in England. *Canadian Medical Association Journal* 1996 Feb 1; 154 (3) : 388-390.

Davidoff F, Haynes B, Sackett D et al. Evidence based medicine : a new journal to help doctors identify the information they need. *British Medical Journal* 1995; 310 (6987) : 1085-6

Deighan M and Boyd K. Defining evidence-based health care : a health-care learning strategy *NT Research* 1996; 1 (5) : 332-339.

Dickersin K and Herxheimer A (eds). The quality of the medical evidence : is it good enough? *International Journal of Technology Assessment in Health Care* 1996 Spring; 12 (2) : 187-287.

Evidence-Based Care Resource Group. Evidence-based care : 1. Setting priorities : how important is this problem? *Canadian Medical Association Journal* 1994 Apr 15; 150 (8) : 1249-1254

Evidence-Based Care Resource Group. Evidence-based care : 2. Setting guidelines : how should we manage this problem? *Canadian Medical Association Journal* 1994 May 1; 150 (9) : 1417-1423.

Evidence-Based Care Resource Group. Evidence-based care : 3. Measuring performance : how are we managing this problem? *Canadian Medical Association Journal* 1994 May 15; 150 (10) : 1575-1579.

Evidence-Based Care Resource Group. Evidence-based care : 4. Improving performance : how can we improve the way we manage this problem? *Canadian Medical Association Journal* 1994 Jun 1; 150 (11) : 1793-1796.

Evidence-Based Care Resource Group. Evidence-based care : 5. Lifelong learning : how can we learn to be more effective? *Canadian Medical Association Journal* 1994 Jun 15; 150 (12): 1971-1973.

Evidence-Based Medicine Working Group. Evidence-based medicine : a new approach to teaching the practice of medicine. *JAMA* 1992; 268 (17) : 2420-2425. Also available on the Internet as : ***http://HIRU.MCMASTER.CA/ebm/overview.htm.***

Glasziou PP and Irwig LM. An evidence based approach to individualising treatment. *British Medical Journal* 1995 Nov 18;311 (7016) : 1356-1359

Haines M (ed). Special Issue on "Current issues in Evidence-based Practice". *Health Libraries Review* 1994 December; 11 (4).

Hunter DJ. Evidence-Based Medicine : the illusion of certainty. *IFMH Inform* 1996 Autumn/Winter; 7 (3) : 1-2.

Hunter DJ. Rationing and evidence-based medicine. *Journal of Evaluation in Clinical Practice* 1996 February; 2 (1) : 5-8

Lowry F. Computers a cornerstone of evidence-based care, conference told. *Canadian Medical Association Journal* 1995; 153 (11) : 1636-1639

Macpherson DW. Evidence Based Medicine (reprinted from *Canada Communicable Disease Report*, 1994; 20 : 145-147). *Canadian Medical Association Journal*, 1995, 152 (2) : 201-202.

Rees J. Rethinking consultants - Where medical science and human behavior meet. *British Medical Journal* 1995; 310 (6983) : 850-853.

Richardson WS; Wilson MC; Nishikawa J et al. The well-built clinical question : a key to evidence-based decisions [editorial]. *ACP Journal Club* 1995 Nov-Dec; 123 (3) : A12-A13.

Rosenberg W and Donald A. Evidence based medicine : an approach to clinical problem-solving *British Medical Journal* 1995 Apr 29; 310 (6987) : 1122-1126.

Rosenberg WMC and Sackett DL. On the need for evidence-based medicine. *Therapie* 1996; 51 (3) : 212-217.

Sackett DL. Applying overviews and meta-analyses at the bedside. *Journal of Clinical Epidemiology* 1995; 48 (1) : 61-66.

Sackett DL and Haynes RB. On the need for evidence-based medicine. *Evidence-Based Medicine* 1995; 1 (1) : 5-6

Sackett DL and Rosenberg WMC. Evidence based medicine & guidelines. In : *Clinical effectiveness : from guidelines to cost-effective practice*. Deighan M & Hitch S. (eds). Brentwood, Essex : Earlybrave Publications Limited, 1995.

Sackett DL and Rosenberg WMC. On the need for evidence-based medicine [editorial]. *Health Economics.* 1995 Jul-Aug; 4 (4) : 249-254.

Sackett DL and Rosenberg WMC. On the need for evidence-based medicine. *Journal of Public Health Medicine.* 1995 Sep; 17 (3) : 330-334

Sackett DL and Rosenberg WMC. The need for evidence-based medicine. *Journal of the Royal Society of Medicine.* 1995 Nov; 88 (11) : 620-624

Sackett DL, Rosenberg WMC , Muir Gray JA et al. Evidence based medicine : what it is and what it isn't. *British Medical Journal* 1996 Jan 13; 312 (7023) : 71-72.(See also the **http://cebm.jr2.ox.ac.uk/ebmisisnt.html** Web version of this paper)

Smith R. The ethics of ignorance. *Journal of Medical Ethics* 1992; 18 : 117-118.

Taubes G. Looking for the evidence in medicine [news] *Science.* 1996 Apr 5; 272(5258) : 22-24

Vines G. Is there a database in the house? *New Scientist* 1995 Jan 21st; 14-15.

Walshe K, Ham C and Appleby J. Given in evidence. *Health Service Journal* 1995; 105 (5459) : 28-29.

Walshe K. Evidence-based health care : brave new world? *Health Care Risk Report* 1996 Mar; 2 (4) : 16-18.

Comments and Critiques

Ahmed T and Silagy C. The move towards Evidence-Based Medicine [editorial] . *Medical Journal of Australia* 1995; 163 (2) : 60-61. [Correspondence by O'Rourke MF and Reply by Ahmed and Silagy in *Medical Journal Of Australia*, 1995, 163 (6) : 332]

Barer D. Narrative or systematic reviews : can we be more 'evidence based'? *Reviews in Clinical Gerontology* 1995; 5 (4) : 365.

Batstone G and Edwards M. Evidence-based practice : converts, cynics and those in between. *Journal of Clinical Effectiveness* 1996; 1(4) : 123.

Bayley H. When the doctor doesn't know best. *New Statesman & Society* 1995; 8 (376) : 30.

Beckbornholdt HP and Dubben HH. Is gambling a serious alternative to Evidence-Based Medicine - rebuttal (Correspondence). *Radiotherapy and Oncology* 1995; 35 (2) : 161-162.

Black N. Why we need observational studies to evaluate the effectiveness of health care. *British Medical Journal* 1996 May 11; 312 (7040) : 1215-1218.

Boissel JP, Collet JP and Dupuy C. Evidence-based medicine or how to realize an important evolution in clinical practice. *Therapie* 1996; 51 (3) : 207-208.

Bouvenot G. Evidence-Based Medicine. *Therapie* 1996; 51 (3) : 209-211.

Browning R. Reinventing the wheel : is the rising support for Evidence Based Medicine a case of deja-vu? *Pharmaceutical Times -London* 1996 Aug; 21.

Buckley NA, McDonald JA, Foy-H et al. Is Wednesday's child filled with woe? An evidence-based reassessment [letter]. *Medical Journal of Australia.* 1995 Dec 4-18; 163(11-12) : 654

Carr-Hill R. Welcome? to the brave new world of Evidence Based Medicine [editorial]. *Social Science and Medicine* 1995 Dec; 41 (11) : 1467-68.

Carroll L. Evidence-Based Medicine - Terminologic lapse or terminologic arrogance. *American Journal of Cardiology* 1996; 78 (5) : 608-609.

Charlton B. The limits of evidence based medicine [editorial]. *Hospital Update* 1996 Jul; 268-269.

Clancy, C.M. & Kamerow, D.B. (1996) Evidence-based medicine meets cost-effectiveness analysis. *JAMA* 1996 Jul 24-31; 276 (4) : 329-330

Correspondence - Evidence-based medicine. [Reply by Sackett D and 8 other letters in reply to Ellis (1995)]. *Lancet* 1995 Sep 23; 346 (8978), : 837-841.

Correspondence - Evidence-based medicine. *Lancet* 1995; 346 (8983) (Evidence-based medicine - Shahar-E and Evidence-based medicine - Morgan WK and Evidence-based medicine and Kurt Godel - Sleigh JW and. Evidence-based medicine - Marshall T and Evidence-based medicine - Sackett D and Evidence-based medicine - Haynes B, pp. 1171-1172).

Correspondence. Evidence-based medicine. *Lancet* 1995 Nov 11; 346 (8985) : 1300.(Evidence-based medicine - Norman-G and Evidence-based medicine - Blau-JN, p. 1300).

Correspondence. *British Medical Journal* 1995; 311 (6999) (Evidence Based Medicine : example was flawed - Fitzmaurice DA, and Evidence Based Medicine : Megatrials are subordinate to medical science -Charlton BG and Evidence Based Medicine : must be applied critically - Griffiths M, and Evidence Based Medicine : many questions cannot be answered by Evidence Based Medicine - Dearlove O et al and Evidence Based Medicine : No guidance is provided for situations for which evidence is lacking - Jones GW, Sagar SM, and Evidence Based Medicine : quality cannot always be quantified - Smith BH and Evidence Based Medicine : *Journal of Evaluation in Clinical Practice* will start publication in September - Miles A, and Evidence Based Medicine : Accurate references are important - Mitchell ABS and Evidence Based Medicine : reply - Rosenberg W and Donald A, pp. 257-9)

Correspondence - Evidence-based medicine : Commentaries should be evidence based too. *British Medical Journal* 1996 Feb 10; 312 (7027) : 380. [Pearson NJ; Sarangi J and Fey R; Reply:- Sackett DL et al].

Correspondence - Evidence based medicine debated. *Lancet* 1996 May 18; 347 (9012) : 1326. [Schuchman M].

Correspondence - *British Medical Journal*. 1996 Jun 22; 312(7046). Evidence-based medicine : letters pages are essential for peer review - Spodick-DH and Reply. Haynes RB, Sackett DL. and Evidence-based medicine : reviews may not be sufficiently critical of evidence - Rao JN and Middleton JD, Reply. Absher JR. , pp. 1610-1611).

Correspondence - Evidence-based medicine and compassion. *Lancet*. 1996 Jun 29; 347 (9018) : 1839 [Newton J and West E].

Correspondence - Minerva's comment was not evidence based *British Medical Journal*. 1996 Jul 13; 313 (7049) : 113 [De Ruysscher D; Specenier P; Spaas P].

Correspondence *British Medical Journal*. 1996 Jul 20; 313(7050) (Evidence based medicine : cost effectiveness and equity are ignored - Maynard A. and Evidence based medicine : needs to be within framework of decision making based on decision analysis - Dowie J and Evidence based medicine : authors' redefinition is better but not perfect - Dearlove OR; Rogers J; and Sharples A and Evidence based medicine : scientific method and raw data should be considered - James NT and Evidence based medicine : rich sources of evidence are ignored - Smith BH, pp. 169-171).

Coulter A. Evidence-based practice : a joint endeavour. *IHSM Network* 1996 Mar; 3 (6) : 1. [Notes that little progress has been made so far in developing strategies for evidence based practice].

Court C. *NHS Handbook* criticizes evidence-based medicine. *British Medical Journal*, 1996, 312 (7044) : 1439-1440.

David Sackett calls for the use of evidence-based medicine and cost-utility information to increase public confidence in a just NHS. *OHE News* 1996 Spring; (3) : 1,11 [Content of the Office of Health Economics annual lecture, 1996, given by Professor Sackett].

Davidoff F. I've been over into the future... *Annals of Internal Medicine* 1995; 123 (8) : 629.

Davidoff F, Case K, and Fried PW. Evidence-based Medicine : why all the fuss? [Editorial]. *Annals of Internal Medicine* 1995; 122 (9) : 727.

Dowie J. Evidence-based medicine - needs to be within framework of decision-making based on decision-analysis. *British Medical Journal* 1996; 313 (7050) : 170

Dowie J. "Evidence-based", "cost effective" and "preference-driven" medicine : decision analysis based medical decision making is the pre-requisite. *Journal of Health Services Research and Policy* 1996 Apr; 1(2) : 104-113.

Down End Research Group. Polythenia gravis : the downside of evidence based medicine.. *British Medical Journal* 1995 Dec 23-30; 311 (7021) : 1666-1668.

Drife OJ. Evidence farm. *British Medical Journal* 1995; 311 : 1375.

Evans JG. Evidence-based and evidence-biased medicine [commentary]. *Age and Ageing* 1995 Nov; 24 (6) : 461-3.

Evidence-based medicine, in its place [editorial]. *Lancet* 1995; 346 (8978) : 785.

Feussner JR. Evidence-based medicine - new priority for an old paradigm. *Journal of Bone and Mineral Research* 1996; 11 (7) : 877-882

Flood AB. Scientific bases versus scientism in health services. *Journal of Health Services Research and Policy* 1996; 1 (2) : 63-64

Freemantle N. Dealing with uncertainty : will science solve the problems of resource allocation in the UK NHS? *Social Science and Medicine* 1995; 40 (10) : 1365-70.

Freemantle N. Are decisions taken by health care professionals rational? A non systematic review of experimental and quasi experimental literature.*Health Policy* 1996; 38 (2) : 71

Glasziou PP and Delmar CB. ABC Series may be anachronistic in era of Evidence Based Medicine. *British Medical Journal*, 1996; 313 (7061) : 880.

Grahame-Smith D : Evidence based medicine : Socratic dissent. *British Medical Journal* 1995; 310:1126-1127.

Grayson L. The burden of evidence. *IFMH Inform* 1996; 7 (3) : 9-13.

Greenhalgh T. "Is my practice evidence-based? : should be answered in qualitative as well as quantitative terms. *British Medical Journal* 1996 Oct 19; 313 (7063) : 957-958.

Haines A et al. Innovations in service and the appliance of science. *British Medical Journal* 1995; 310 : 815-816.

Hope T. Evidence based medicine and ethics [editorial]. *Journal of Medical Ethics* 1995 Oct; 21 (5) : 259-260.

Horwitz RI The dark side of Evidence-Based Medicine. *Cleveland Clinic Journal of Medicine* 1996; 63 (6) : 320-323.

Hunter D. Evidence-based medicine is no panacea. *Health Director* 1996 Jun; (29) : 12-13.

Hunter DJ. Evidence-based medicine and rational rationing. *Journal of Clinical Effectiveness* 1996; 1 (4) : 124-128.

Hutton JL. The ethics of randomized controlled trials : a matter of statistical belief? *Health Care Analysis* 1996 May; 4 (2) : 95-102.

Hyde CJ. Using the evidence. *International Journal of Technology Assessment in Health Care* 1996; 12 : 280-287.

Jadad AR. "Are you playing evidence-based medicine games with our daughter?" (Correspondence). *Lancet* 1996 Jan 27; 347 (8996) : 274.

Lamont-Gregory E, Henry CJK and Ryan TJ. Evidence-based humanitarian relief interventions (correspondence). *Lancet* 1995; 346 (8970) : 312-313

Laupacis A. Preventive therapies : weighing the pros and cons [editorial; comment]. *Canadian Medical Association Journal.* 1996 May 15; 154(10) : 1510-1512.

Maynard A. Evidence-based medicine : an incomplete method for informing treatment choices. *Lancet* Jan 11; 349 (9045) : 126-128.

Moran N. Treatment choices from Evidence-Based Medicine [editorial]. *Nature Medicine,* 1995; 1 (11) : 1114-1115

Naylor CD. Grey zones of clinical practice : some limits to evidence-based medicine. *Lancet* 1995 Apr 1; 345 (8953) : 840-842.

Polychronis A, Miles A and Bentley P. Evidence-based medicine : reference? dogma? neologism? new orthodoxy? *Journal of Evaluation in Clinical Practice* 1996 Feb; 2 (1) : 1-3

Polychronis A, Miles A and Bentley P. The protagonists of evidence-based medicine : arrogant, seductive and controversial. *Journal of Evaluation in Clinical Practice* 1996 Feb; 2 (1) : 9-12

Romero LG. Medicine based on evidence - An attempt to bring science together with the art of clinical practice. *Medicina Clinica,* 1996; 107 (10) : 377-382

Schuchman M. Evidence-based medicine debated. *Lancet* 1996 May 18; 347 (9012) : 1396

Smith AFM. Mad cows and ecstasy : chance and choice in an evidence-based society. *Journal of the Royal Statistical Society Series A.* 1996; 159 : 367-383.

Smith R. Where is the wisdom? the poverty of medical evidence [editorial] *British Medical Journal* 1991; 303 : 798-799.

Smith R and Rennie D. And now, evidence based editing [editorial]. *British Medical Journal.* 1995 Sep 30; 311(7009) : 826

Smith T. Evidence based politics. *British Medical Journal* 1996; 312 (7023) : 127.

Summers RI. Evidence-based medicine versus scientific reasoning. *Academic Emergency Medicine* 1996; 3(2) : 183-184.

Swales J. Science and medical practice : the turning tide. *Journal of Health Services Research and Policy* 1996; 1 (2) : 61.

Walker ARP and Labadarios D. Evidence-based medicine : how much does it explain? *South African Medical Journal* 1996; 86 (8) : 939-940

Walker ARP and Labadarios D. Evidence-based medicine - What part does it play in combating nutritional deficiencies and excesses? *South African Medical Journal* 1996 : 86 (4) 454-456.

West R. Assessment of evidence versus consensus or prejudice. *Journal of Epidemiology and Community Health* 1992; 46 (4) : 321-2.

Wise J. A body of evidence to boost efficiency. *Hospital Doctor* 1995 May 18; 34.

EVIDENCE BASED HEALTH CARE - BIBLIOGRAPHIES

Chartered Society of Physiotherapy. *Evidence based health care : useful references and sources of information.* (Research No. 6). London : CSP, 1996.

Clinical Audit Information Service, Royal College of Nursing and Royal College of Midwives. *Evidence based practice and clinical effectiveness* (Bibliography Series No. 10). London : RCN/RCM, 1996.

EVIDENCE BASED HEALTH CARE - SPECIALTIES

Alternative Medicine

Stalker DF. Evidence and alternative medicine. *Mount Sinai Journal of Medicine* 1995; 62 (2): 132.

Audit

Baker R. Towards evidence based audit. *Audit Trends* 1995; 3 (4) : 117-118.

Critical Care

Boulton F. Evidence based transfusion policies. *Clinician In Management* 1996; 5 (4) : 7.

Cook DJ, Meade MO and Fink MP. How to keep up with the critical care literature and avoid being buried alive. *Critical Care Medicine* 1996 Oct; 24 (10) : 1757-1768.

Cook DJ, Sibbald WJ, Vincent JL et al. Evidence based critical care medicine : What is it and what can it do for us? Evidence Based medicine in critical care group. *Critical Care Medicine* 1996 Feb; 24 (2) : 334-337.

Cooper AB, Doig GS and Sibbald WJ. Pulmonary artery catheters in the critically ill - an overview using the methodology of Evidence-Based Medicine. *Critical Care Clinics* 1996; 12 (4):777

Heyland DK, Kernerman P, Gafni A et al. Economic evaluations in the critical care literature : do they help us improve the efficiency of our unit? *Critical Care Medicine* 1996; 24 (9) : 1591-1598.

Rainer TH and Robertson CE. Adrenaline, cardiac arrest, and Evidence Based Medicine. *Journal of Accident & Emergency Medicine* 1996; 13 (4) : 234-237

Roberts I, Alderson P and Rowan K. Intensive care of severely head-injured patients - guidelines should be based on systematic reviews of the evidence. *British Medical Journal* 1996; 313 (7052) : 297

Sibbald WJ and Inman KJ. Problems in assessing the technology of critical care medicine. *International Journal of Technology Assessment in Health Care* 1992; 8 (3) : 419-443.

Dentistry

Anonymous. Evidence-based health care : a new approach to teaching the practice of health care. Evidence-Based Medicine Working Group. *Journal of Dental Education.* 1994 Aug; 58 (8) : 648-653. [Also see comment in : *Journal of Dental Education* 1994 Aug;58 (8):654-6

Fallowfield M. Evidence based assessment? *British Dental Journal* 1996 Apr 20;180 (8) : 281-282.

International Journal of Periodontics and Restorative Dentistry 1995 Apr; 15(2) : Whole Issue. 116-200. Includes:- Translating clinical outcomes to patient value : an evidence-based treatment approach - Levine RA and Shanaman RH (pp. 186-200), Guided bone regeneration of bone defects associated with implants : an evidence-based outcome assessment - Mellonig-JT and Nevins-M (pp. 168-85), Successful regeneration of mandibular Class II furcation defects : an evidence-based treatment approach - Machtei EE and Schallhorn RG (pp. 146-67), Periodontal regeneration of intrabony defects : an evidence-based treatment approach - Cortellini P and Bowers GM (pp. 128-45) and Evidence-based periodontal treatment. II. Predictable regeneration treatment. Newman MG and McGuire MK (pp. 116-127).

McGuire MK. and Newman MG. Evidence-based periodontal treatment .1. A strategy for clinical decisions. *International Journal of Periodontics & Restorative Dentistry,* 1995 Feb; 15 (1) : 71-83.

McGuire-MK; Newman-MG and Whitley-N Evidence-based periodontal regenerative therapy. *Current Opinion in Periodontology.* 1996; 3 : 109-17

Richards D. Developing evidence based dentistry. *Primary Dental Care* 1996; 3 : 4-5.

Richards D. A centre for evidence-based dentistry. *Journal of Clinical Effectiveness* 1996; 1 (2) : 70-71.

Richards D and Lawrence A. Evidence based dentistry. *British Dental Journal* 1995 Oct 7; 179 (7) : 270-273.

Education

Caudill TS et al. The need for curricula in Evidence-Based Medicine [letter]. *Academic Medicine,* 1995; 70 (9) : 746-747.

Perrett K, Silcocks P, Dixon RA et al : Towards a knowledge based health service. Teaching evidence based medicine in Sheffield. *British Medical Journal* 1994;309 (6956):740-741.

van der Vleuten C. Evidence-based education? [editorial]. *American Journal of Physiology.* 1995 Dec; 269(6 Pt 3) : S3

Williams PL. Evidence based training : the future role of diagnostic radiographers. *British Journal of Radiology* 1996 May; 69 (Suppl)

General Medicine

Cowie MR and Hardman SMC. Heart-failure and angiotensin-converting enzyme-inhibitors : towards evidence-based health-care [editorial]. *British Journal of Hospital Medicine,* 1995, 53 (5) : 186-188.

Ellis J, Mulligan I, Rowe J et al. Inpatient general medicine is evidence based. *Lancet* 1995 Aug 12; 346 (8972) : 407-410.

Elwood JM. Breast cancer screening in younger women - the need for Evidence Based Medicine. *New Zealand Medical Journal* 1995; 108 (1002) : 239-241

Gray TA, Freedman DB, Burnett D et al. Evidence based practice : clinicians' use and attitudes to near patient testing in hospitals. *Journal of Clinical Pathology* 1996; 49 (11) : 903.

Jackson R and Beaglehole R. Evidence-based management of dyslipidemia [editorial] . *Lancet* 1995 Dec 2; 346 (8988) : 1440-1442.

Langhorne P. Developing comprehensive stroke services : an Evidence-based approach. *Postgraduate Medical Journal,* 1995 Dec; 71 (842) : 733-737.

Marchioli R, Marfisi RM, Carinci F et al. Meta-analysis, clinical trials, and transferability of research results into practice. The case of cholesterol-lowering interventions in the secondary prevention of coronary heart disease. *Archives of Internal Medicine.* 1996 Jun 10; 156 (11) : 1158-72

Oparil S. Antihypertensive therapy in the era of evidence based medical practice : what to do until the facts are in . *Current Opinion in Nephrology and Hypertension* 1996; 5 (2) : 159.

General Practice

Bailey J. Evidence-Based Medicine and Primary Care. *IFMH Inform* 1996; 7 (3) : 5-8.

Bjorndal A. Evidence Based Practice [editorial] . *Scandinavian Journal Of Primary Health Care* 1995, 13 (1) : 1-2

Bower P. Where is the evidence for the care you offer? *Fundholding* 1996 Feb 7th; 5 (3) : 35-36. [Explains why GP fundholders should want to be involved in R&D and how such involvement is facilitated and encouraged].

Correspondence GP's management of acute back pain. Is evidence based *British Medical Journal.* 1996 Jun 8; 312(7044) : 1480 [Summerton N].

Correspondence *British Medical Journal.* 1996 Jul 13; 313(7049) (Evidence based general practice. Studies using more sophisticated methods are needed - Meakin R; Lloyd M; and Ward S and Evidence based general practice. Findings of study should prompt debate - Chikwe J and Evidence based general practice. Drug treatment in general practice in Japan is evidence based - Tsuruoka K; Tsuruoka Y; Yoshimura M et al, pp. 114-5).

Dawes MG. On the need for evidence-based general and family practice. *Evidence Based Medicine* 1996 Mar/Apr; 1 (3) : 68-69.

Earl-Slater A et al. Evidence-based prescribing in primary care. *Primary Care Management* 1996; 6 (6) : 6-10

Elmslie T. Integrating research findings into the clinical setting through the practice of evidence-based family medicine. In : Dunn EV et al. *Disseminating Research/Changing Practice.* (Research Methods for Primary Care). London : Sage, 1994.

Gill P, Dowell AC, Neal RD et al. Evidence based general practice : a retrospective study of interventions in one training practice. *British Medical Journal* 1996 Mar 30; 312 (7034) : 819-821.

Hutchinson A, McIntosh A, Roberts A et al. Evidence based health care : the challenge for general practice. In : Deighan M and Hitch S (eds). *Clinical Effectiveness : from guidelines to cost-effective practice.* Brentwood, Essex : Earlybrave Publications Limited, 1995. [ISBN : 1-900432-00-5] : 49-52.

Lawrence M et al.(eds). *Prevention of cardiovascular disease : an evidence-based approach.* (Oxford General Practice series; no. 33). Oxford : Oxford University Press, 1996.

Lewith GT. The use and abuse of evidence based medicine : an example from general practice. *Perfusion* 1995; 8 (11) : 375.

Lim TK. Asthma practice guidelines : common sense, expert opinion or evidence based approach? *Singapore Medical Journal* 1996; 37 (4) : 340

Little P, Smith L, Cantrell T et al. General practitioners' management of acute back pain : a survey of reported practice compared with clinical guidelines. *British Medical Journal.* 1996 Feb 24; 312 (7029) : 485-488.

North of England evidence based guidelines development project : summary version of evidence based guideline for the primary care management of angina. North of England Stable Angina Guideline Development Group. *British Medical Journal.* 1996 Mar 30; 312 (7034) : 827-32

North of England evidence based guidelines development project : summary version of evidence based guideline for the primary care management in adults. North of England Asthma Guideline Development Group. *British Medical Journal.* 1996 Mar 23; 312 (7033) : 762-6

Ridsdale L. *Evidence-based general practice : a critical reader.* London : W B Saunders, 1995.

Ringel SP and Hughes RI. Evidence-Based Medicine, Critical Pathways, Practice Guidelines, and Managed Care - reflections on the prevention and care of stroke. *Archives of Neurology* 1996, 53 (9) : 867-871

Taylor RJ. Experts and evidence [editorial]. *British Journal of General Practice* 1996 May; 46 (406) : 268-270.

Williams S and McIntosh J. Problems in implementing evidence-based health promotion material in general practice. *Health Education Journal* 1996; 55 (1) : 24-30.

Wise J. Time for GPs to scrutinise the evidence. *Doctor* 1995 May 25; 25.

Wood FE et al. General practitioners and information : evidence based practice explored. In:- *Current perspectives in healthcare computing, Harrogate 18-20 March 1996*, edited by B Richards. Weybridge : BJHC, 1996 : 543-550. [ISBN 0-948198-24-9]

Nursing

Cullum N. *The identification and systematic review of randomized controlled trials in nursing.* York, Centre for Health Economics, University of York, 1995.

Cullum N and Sheldon T. Clinically challenged : The importance of evidence based health care. *Nursing Management* 1996; 3 (4) : 14-16.

Dickson R and Droogan J (eds) for the NHS Centre for Reviews and Dissemination. *Systematic reviews: examples for nursing.* London : RCN Publishing Company, 1997. [Copies of this booklet are available price £ 2.50 (includ. p&p) from Nursing Standard Mail Order, RCN Publishing Company, PO Box 33, NEWPORT, Gwent NP1 4YN.

Shuldham C and Hiley C. Randomised controlled trials in clinical practice: the continuing debate. *NT Research* 1997; 2 (2) : 128-134.

Obstetrics and Gynaecology

Grimes DA. Introducing evidence-based medicine into a Department of Obstetrics and Gynecology. *Obstetrics and Gynecology* 1995; 86 : 451-457.

Elkins TE, Gabert HA, Braly PS et al. Introducing evidence-based medicine into a Department of Obstetrics and Gynecology. *Obstetrics and Gynecology* 1996 Jan; 87 (1) : 159-160. [Reply - Grimes DA, p. 160]

Enkin MW. The need for evidence-based obstetrics. *Evidence Based Medicine* 1996 Jul/Aug; 1 (5) : 132-133.

Grant J.M. Multicentre trials in obstetrics and gynaecology : smaller explanatory trials are required. *British Journal of Obstetrics & Gynaecology* 1996 Jul; 103 (7) : 599-602.

King JC and Kovac-SR. Evidence-based practice in obstetrics and gynecology : its time has come [letter]. *American Journal of Obstetrics and Gynecology.* 1996 Jul; 175(1) : 232-3

Sackett DL and Cooke IE. *Evidence-based Obstetrics and Gynaecology.* London : Bailliere Tindall, 1997. [ISBN : 0702022608]

Thacker SB, Peterson HB and Stroup DF. Metaanalysis for the Obstetrician-Gynecologist. *American Journal of Obstetrics and Gynecology,* 1996, 174 (5) : 1403-1407.

Ophthalmology

Fielder AR and Quinn GE. Evidently, evidence based. *British Journal of Ophthalmology,* 1996; 80 (4) : 273

Paediatrics and Child Health

Gilbert R and Logan S. Evidence-based child health and the health care research and development industry. *Journal of Clinical Effectiveness* 1996; 1 (4) : 146-148.

Gilbert RE and Logan S. Future prospects for evidence-based child health. *Archives of Disease in Childhood* (In press)

Perinatology

Martin GI. Neonatology by rumor or reality : evidence-based decision making [editorial] *Journal of Perinatology*. 1995 Jul-Aug; 15(4) : 263

Ohlsson A. Randomized controlled trials and systematic reviews : a foundation for evidence-based perinatal medicine. *Acta Paediatrica* 1996; 85 (6) : 647-655.

Seminars in Perinatology 1995; 19 (2) : Whole Issue on Evidence Based Perinatology.

Sinclair FC. Systematic reviews of Randomized Trials in Neonatology. *Current Topics In Neonatology*, 1996; 1 : 135

Pharmacology and Toxicology

Buckley NA and Smith AJ. Evidence-based medicine in toxicology : where is the evidence? *Lancet* 1996 Apr 27; 347 (9009) : 1167-1169.

Collet JP. Evidence based medicine and drug prescription - reasons for discrepancy. *Therapie* 1996; 51 (3) : 221-224

Li Wan Po A. Evidence based pharmacotherapy. *Pharmaceutical Journal* 1996 Mar 2; 256 (6881) : 308-312.

Physiotherapy and Occupational Therapy

Bury T. Evidence-based practice : survival of the fittest. *Physiotherapy* 1996; 82(2) : 75-76.

Culshaw HMS. Evidence-based practice for sale? *British Journal of Occupational Therapy* 1995; 58 (6) : 233.

Durward B and Baer G. Physiotherapy and neurology : towards research-based practice. *Physiotherapy* 1995; 81 (8) : 436-439.

Harrison MA. Evidence-based practice - practice-based evidence. *Physiotherapy Theory and Practice* 1996 Sep; 12 (3) : 129-130

Jackson DA, Llewelyn-Phillips H and Klaber-Moffett JA. Categorization of back pain patients using an evidence based approach. *Musculoskeletal Management* 1996 Nov; 2 (1) : 39-46.

Mead J. Evidence based practice : how far have we come? *Physiotherapy* 1996; 82 (12) : 653-654.

Partridge C. Evidence based medicine - implications for physiotherapy? *Physiotherapy Research International* 1996; 1 (2), 69-73

Psychiatry and Mental Health

Bilsker D. From evidence to conclusions in psychiatric research. *Canadian Journal Of Psychiatry-Revue Canadienne De Psychiatrie* 1996; 41 (4) : 227-232

Geddes, J. On the need for evidence-based psychiatry. *Evidence-Based Medicine* 1996 Nov-Dec; 1 (7) : 199-200

Geddes J, Game D, Jenkins N et al. In patient psychiatric treatment is evidence-based. *Quality in Health Care* (In press).

Gill DB et al. Randomized controlled trials in the *Journal of Psychosomatic Research*; 1956-1993 : a prevalence study. *Journal of Psychosomatic Research* 1995; 39 (8) : 949-956.

Goldner EM and Bilsker D. Evidence-based psychiatry. *Canadian Journal of Psychiatry* 1995; 40 (2):97-101.

Hunter J, Higginson I and Garralda E. Systematic literature review : outcome measures for child and adolescent mental health services. *Journal of Public Health Medicine*, 1996; 18 (2):197-206

Summers A and Kehoe RF. Is psychiatric treatment evidence-based? [letter] *Lancet* 1996 Feb 10; 347 (8998) : 409-410.

Public Health

Fahey T et al. The type and quality of randomized controlled trials (RCTS) published in UK public health journals. *Journal of Public Health Medicine* 1995; 17 (4) : 469-474.

Mansoor-OD. Immunization : sacred cow or evidence based medicine? [letter]. *New Zealand Medical Journal.* 1996 May 10; 109(1021) : 171-172.

Young Y, Brigley S, Littlejohns P et al. Continuing education for public health medicine - is it just another paper exercise? *Journal of Public Health Medicine* 1996; 18 (3):357-363.

Purchasing, Policy and Management

Armstrong EM, Tremblay M, Azuonye IO. Evidence based policymaking (Correspondence). *British Medical Journal* 1995;310:1141

Barker J. A methodology for evidence based health policy making : The Welsh Protocol Enhancement Project. In : Lloyd-Williams M (ed). *SHIMR 96 : Proceedings of the Second International Symposium on Health Information Management Research.* University of Sheffield, 27-29 March, 1996. Sheffield : Centre for Health Information Management Research, University of Sheffield, 1996.

Dixon S, Booth A and Perrett K. An application of evidence based priority setting in a health authority. *Journal of Public Health Medicine* 1997 Sep; (In press).

Fahey T, Griffiths S and Peters TJ. Evidence based purchasing : understanding results of clinical trials and systematic reviews. *British Medical Journal* 1995 Oct 21;311 (7012):1056-1060.

Farmer J and Chesson R. The informers. *Health Service Journal* 1996 Feb 1; 106 (5488) : 28-29.

Farrell C (ed). *Purchasing evidence-based podiatry/chiropody services : report of a conference organised for the NHS Executive by the King's Fund, December 1995.* London : King's Fund 1995.

Ham C, Hunter DJ and Robinson R. Evidence based policymaking - Research must inform health policy as well as medical care. *British Medical Journal* 1995; 310 (6972):71-72.

Harrison S and Long A (eds). Evidence based decisionmaking. *Health Service Journal.* (Glaxo Wellcome Supplement 6) 1996; 1-12. Includes articles on : The balance of evidence : why evidence-based medicine has become central to health policy : pp. 1-2; An ABC of EBM : practical advice on implementing evidence based decision making : pp 3-4; Case studies : pp. 5-11, and Manager's checklist : five main pointers for implementing an evidence-based approach : 11.

Hayward J. Purchasing clinically effective care. *British Medical Journal* 1994; 309 (6958) : 823-824.

Hunter DJ. Evidence-based medicine and rational rationing. *Journal of Clinical Effectiveness* 1996; 1 (4) : 134-136.

Hunter DJ. Editorial : Rationing and evidence-based medicine. *Journal of Evaluation in Clinical Practice* 1996; 2 (1) : 5-8

Hyde C. Active research dissemination in the West Midlands. *Journal of Clinical Effectiveness* 1996; 1 (1) : 30.

Littlejohns P, Dumelow C and Griffiths S. Knowledge based commissioning : can a national clinical effectiveness policy be compatible with seeking local professional advice. *Journal of Health Services Research and Policy* 1996; 1 : 28-34.

Mackenbach JP. Tackling inequalities in health - great need for Evidence Based interventions [editorial] . *British Medical Journal,* 1995; 310 (6988) : 1152-1153.

Maynard A. Evidence Based Medicine : There's going to be a radical change in healthcare purchasing. *Pharmaceutical Times -London* 1996 Mar; 18.

Miles A, Bentley P, Price N et al. Purchasing quality in clinical practice : precedents and problems. In : Miles A and Lugon M (eds). *Effective clinical practice.* Oxford : Blackwell Science, 1996 : 183-204.

Milne R. Evidence-based purchasing. *Evidence-Based Medicine* 1996 May; 1 (4) : 101-102.

Murray, C.J.L., Lopez, A.D. Evidence-based health policy : lessons from the global burden of disease. *Science* 1996 Nov 1; 274 (5288) : 740

Peach E for the Yorkshire Collaborating Centre for Health Services Research. *Evidence based contracting for health care.* Leeds : University of Leeds, Nuffield Institute for Health, 1995.

Raffle A. Once bitten twice shy : why evidence-based purchasers are right to be cautious about screening. *Evidence-based Purchasing* 1996 May; (13) : 1,4.

Sheldon TA, Raffle A, Watt I. Department of Health shoots itself in the hip : why the report of the Advisory Group on Osteoporosis undermines evidence based purchasing. *British Medical Journal*, 1996 Feb 3; 312 (7026) : 296-297.

Stevens A, Colin-Jones D and Gabbay J. "Quick and clean" : authoritative health technology assessment for local health care contracting. *Health Trends* 1995; 27 : 37-42.

Stocking B. The art and science of medicine. *IHSM Network* 1996 Mar; 3 (6) : 3. [Indicates 3 courses of action that NHS managers should adopt to support moves towards evidence based practice].

Watson P, Horne G and Firth A. Knowing the score. *Health Service Journal* 1996 Mar 14 : 28-31 [Describes how a scoring system helped one purchasing authority assess new services and decide on funding priorities].

Rheumatology

Ferraz MB. An evidence based appraisal of the management of nontophaceous interval gout [editorial]. *Journal of Rheumatology* 1995 Sep; 22 (9) : 1618-1620.

Tannenbaum H, Davis P, Russell AS et al. An evidence-based approach to prescribing NSAIDs in musculoskeletal disease : a Canadian consensus. Canadian NSAID Consensus Participants. *Canadian Medical Association Journal.* 1996 Jul 1; 155(1) : 77-88

CLINICAL EFFECTIVENESS

Alderman C. Sharing a vision : Clinical effectiveness. *Nursing Standard* 1996; 10 (41) : 22.

Appleby J, Walshe K and Ham C. *Acting on the evidence : a review of clinical effectiveness, sources of information, dissemination and implementation.* (NAHAT Research Paper 17) Birmingham : NAHAT, 1995.

Baker M and Kirk S (eds). *Research and development for the NHS : evidence, evaluation and effectiveness.* Oxford : Radcliffe Medical Press, 1996.

Batstone G and Edwards M. Focusing on clinical effectiveness. *Journal of Clinical Effectiveness*, 1996; 1 (1) : 1.

Batstone G and Edwards M. Achieving clinical effectiveness : just another initiative or a real change in working practice? *Journal of Clinical Effectiveness* 1996; 1 (1) : 19-21.

Deighan M and Hitch S. (eds). *Clinical Effectiveness : from guidelines to cost-effective practice.* Brentwood, Essex : Earlybrave Publications Limited, 1995.

Department of Health. *Research and development : towards an evidence-based health service.* London : Department of Health, February 1995.

Department of Health. *Next step in drive to promote clinical effectiveness.* Press Release 1996 Jan 10 : (96/5).

Dimond B. Burden of proof : if we're not sure about the effectiveness of a treatment, why should we expect it to be funded? *Health Service Journal* 1996 Nov 14; 106 (5529). Law Special Report. 11.

Dunning M and Cooper S. Setting the PACE. *Health Director* 1996; (29) : 1011.

Dunning M and and Holmes J. PACE : promoting action on clinical effectiveness. *IHSM Network* 1996 Mar; 3 (6) : 4. [Introduces PACE (Promoting Action on Clinical Effectiveness) the King's Fund's new research programme which is intended to help change practice and develop evidence based health services].

Evans D. Commitment to a targeted approach to effectiveness in North Thames. *Purchasing in Practice* 1996 Feb; (7) : 16-17.

Farquhar W. Clinical effectiveness : making it happen. *Audit Trends* 1996; 4 (3) : 85.

Firth-Cozens, J. Looking at effectiveness : ideas from the couch. *Quality in Health Care* 1996; 5 (1), 55-59

Focus on Clinical Effectiveness. *Health Director*, 1996 Jun; 10

Graham G. Clinical effectiveness in a rational health service : Strategic partnerships can make it a reality. *Health Director* 1996 Jun; (22):11-12.

Hayward J. Promoting clinical effectiveness : a welcome initiative, but both clinical and health policy need to be based on evidence.. *British Medical Journal* 1996 Jun 15; 312 : (7045) : 1491-1492. [Reviews the booklet *"Promoting clinical effectiveness : a framework.....*].

Health Education Board for Scotland, Research and Evaluation Division. How effective are effectiveness reviews? *Health Education Journal* 1996; 55 : 359-362.

Hewison A and Weale A. Evidence of local care. *Nursing Management* 1996 Oct; 3 (6) : 8-9.

Hunter DJ. Effective practice. *Journal of Evaluation in Clinical Practice* 1995; 1 (2) : 131-134.

Improving the effectiveness of clinical services. *Purchasing in Practice* 1996 Feb; (7) : 20-21. [Reports on work being done in the DoH's clinical effectiveness programme].

Littlejohns P, Dumelow C and Griffiths S. Implementing a national clinical effectiveness policy : developing relationships between purchasers and clinicians. *Journal of Clinical Effectiveness* 1996; 1 (4) : 124-128.

MacDonald J. Opportunity or threat? *IHSM Network* 1996 Mar; 3 (6) : 5-6. [Outlines the approach being taken by Derbyshire Royal Infirmary and South Derbyshire Health to develop clinical effectiveness through projects funded by the PACE initiative].

Miles A, O'Neill D and Polychronis A. Central dimensions of clinical practice evaluation : efficiency, appropriateness and effectiveness - II. *Journal of Evaluation in Clinical Practice* 1996 May; 2 (2) : 131-152.

Murphy M and Dunning M. Implementing clinical effectiveness - is it time for a change of gear? *British Journal of Health Care Management* 1997; 3 (1) : 23-26.

NHS Executive. *Improving clinical effectiveness.* Leeds : NHS Executive, 1993. (EL(93) 115).

NHS Executive. *Improving the effectiveness of the NHS.* Leeds : NHS Executive, 1994. (EL(94) 74).

NHS Executive. *Improving the effectiveness of clinical services.* Leeds : NHS Executive, 1995. (EL (95) 105).

NHS Executive. *Promoting clinical effectiveness : a framework for action in and through the NHS.* Leeds : NHS Executive; 1996.

NHS machine : New treatments on more than just clinical effectiveness. *Pharmaceutical Marketing -Dorking-* 1996; 8 (3) : 24.

Normand C. The search for evidence of effectiveness. *NT Research* 1996; 1 (4) : 249-250.

Nursing and Midwifery Audit Information Service. *Effectiveness and Evidence Based Practice.* (Factsheet series). London : Royal College of Nursing, 1996.

O'Neill D, Miles A. and Polychronis A. Central dimensions of clinical practice evaluation : efficiency, appropriateness and effectiveness - 1. *Journal of Evaluation in Clinical Practice* 1996 Feb; 2 (1) : 13-27

Roberts C. Lewis P, Crosby D et al. Prove it. *Health Service Journal* 1996 Mar 7; 106 (5493; 32-33. [Questions whether services should be purchased unless assertions about their effectiveness can be tested].

Royal College of Nursing. *Clinical Effectiveness : a Royal College of Nursing Guide.* London : RCN, 1996.

Sharples F. Effectiveness - a complementary view. *Health Director* 1996 Sep; (31) : 4-5. [Describes clinical effectiveness initiative at the Royal London Homeopathic Hospital NHS Trust with complementary therapies for eczema and asthma].

Summerton N. The burden of proof. *Health Service Journal* 1995 Nov 30; 105 (5481):33.

Summerton N. Personal effects. *Health Service Journal* 1996 Feb 29; 106 (5492) : 33.

Turner A. Clinically effective : Nurses need to keep up-to-date with clinical effectiveness. *Nursing Management* 1996 Jul; 3 (4) : 18-19.

Welsh Office. *Towards evidence based practice : a clinical effectiveness initiative for Wales.* Welsh Office May 1995.

Welsh Office. *Helping practitioners use the evidence : clinical effectiveness briefing paper 2.* Welsh Office January 1996.

Walshe K and Appleby J. Given in evidence. *Health Service Journal* 1995 June 29; 28-29.

NHS CENTRE FOR REVIEWS AND DISSEMINATION

Sheldon TA. Research intelligence for policy and practice : the role of the National Health Service Centre for Reviews and Dissemination. *Evidence Based Medicine* 1996 Sep-Oct; 1 (6) : 167-168.

Sheldon TA and Melville A. Providing intelligence for rational decision-making in the NHS : the NHS Centre for Reviews and Dissemination. *Journal of Clinical Effectiveness* 1996; 1 (2) : 51-54.

Watt I. The NHS Centre for Reviews and Dissemination. *The Clinician in Management* 1996 Feb; 5 (1) : 9-11.

LITERATURE SEARCHING

How to harness MEDLINE......

McKibbon KA and Walker CJ. Beyond ACP Journal Club : how to harness MEDLINE for diagnosis problems [editorial]. *ACP Journal Club* 1994 Sep-Oct : A10 (Ann Intern Med 121 Suppl 2). Available on the World Wide Web as :

http://hiru.hirunet.mcmaster.ca/ebm/userguid/3_diag_s.htm

McKibbon KA and Walker CJ. Beyond ACP Journal Club : how to harness MEDLINE for therapy problems [editorial]. *ACP Journal Club* 1994 Jul-Aug : A10 (Ann Intern Med 121 Suppl 1). Available on the World Wide Web as :

http://hiru.hirunet.mcmaster.ca/ebm/userguid/2_ther_s.htm

McKibbon KA and Walker-Dilks CJ. Beyond ACP Journal Club : how to harness MEDLINE to solve clinical problems [editorial]. *ACP Journal Club* 1994 Mar-Apr : A10-A12 (Ann Intern Med 120 Suppl 2)

McKibbon KA, Walker-Dilks CJ, Wilczynskl NL et al. Beyond ACP Journal Club how to harness MEDLINE for review articles [editorial]. *ACP Journal Club* 1996 May-Jun : A12-13.

Walker-Dilks CJ, McKibbon KA and Haines RB. Beyond ACP Journal Club : how to harness MEDLINE for prognosis problems [editorial]. *ACP Journal Club* 1995 Jul-Aug : A12-A14. (*Ann Intern Med* 123, Suppl 1)

Walker-Dilks CJ, McKibbon KA and Haines RB. Beyond ACP Journal Club : how to harness MEDLINE for etiology problems [editorial]. *ACP Journal Club* 1994 Nov-Dec : A10-11 (*Ann Intern Med* 121 Suppl 3)

Other items

Adams CE, Power A, Frederick K and Lefebvre C. An investigation of the adequacy of MEDLINE searches for randomized controlled trials (RCTs) of the effects of mental health care. *Psychological Medicine* 1994; 24(3) : 741-748.

Brettle A and Grant MJ. Searching the literature on outcomes measurement : a guide to MEDLINE and CINAHL. *Outcomes Briefing* 1996 Oct : (8) : 44-48.

Cahn MA. Practice guidelines : a piece of the quality puzzle. *Bulletin of the Medical Library Association* 1994; 82 (3) : 312-314.

Clarke M and Greaves L : Identifying relevant studies for systematic reviews. *British Medical Journal* 1995; 310 (6981):741

Cooke IE. Finding the evidence. *Bailliere's Clinical Obstetrics and Gynaecology* 1996 Dec; 10 (4) : 551-567.

Counsell C and Fraser H. Identifying relevant studies for systematic reviews. *British Medical Journal* 1995; 310 (6972):126

Dickersin K, Higgins K and Meinert CL. Identification of meta-analyses. The need for standard terminology. *Controlled Clinical Trials* 1990 Feb; 11 (1) 52-66.

Dickersin K, Scherer R and Lefebvre C. Identification of relevant studies for systematic reviews. *British Medical Journal* 1994 Nov 12; 309 (6964) : 1286-1291.

Getzsce PC and Lange B. Comparison of search strategies for recalling double-blind trials from Medline. *Danish Medical Bulletin* 1991; 38:476-8.

Goodman C. *Literature searching and evidence interpretation for assessing health care practices*. Sweden : Stockholm, 1993.

Hay PJ, Adams CE and Lefebvre C. The efficiency of searches for randomized controlled trials in the International Journal of Eating Disorders : a comparison of handsearching, EMBASE and PSYCLIT. *Health Libraries Review* 1996 Jun; 13 (2) : 91-96.

Haynes RB, Wilczynski N, McKibbon KA et al. Developing optimal search strategies for detecting clinically sound studies in MEDLINE. *Journal of the American Medical Informatics Association* 1994; 1(6) : 447-458.

Hunt DL and McKibbon KA. Locating and appraising systematic reviews. *Annals of Internal Medicine* 1997 Apr 1; 126 : 532-538.

Indexing clinical trials in EMBASE. *Profile : Excerpta Medica Newsletter* 1994; (11) : 2.

Jadad AR and McQuay HJ. Searching the literature : be systematic in your searching. *British Medical Journal* 1993 Jul 3; 307(6895) : 66.

Jadad AR and McQuay HJ. A high-yield strategy to identify randomised controlled trials for systematic reviews. *Online Journal of Current Clinical Trials* [serial online] 1993; Doc No 33 : 3973 words; 39 paragraphs.

Knipschild P. Systematic reviews : some examples. *British Medical Journal* 1994;309:719-721

Kuller AB. Quality filtering of the clinical literature by librarians and physicians. *Bulletin of Medical Library Association* 1993; 81 (1) : 38-43.

Lefebvre C. Difficulties in identifying articles in MEDLINE using indexing terms (MeSH) : experience based on attempts to identify reports of randomized controlled trials. *IFM Healthcare Newsletter* 1994 Summer; 5 (2) : 10-15.

Lefebvre C. The Cochrane Collaboration : the role of the UK Cochrane Centre in identifying the evidence. *Health Libraries Review* 1994; 11 (4) : 235-242.

Long AF, Brettle A, and Mercer G. *Searching the literature on the efficacy and effectiveness of complementary therapies*. Leeds University : Yorkshire Collaborating Centre for Health Services Research, 1995.

Lowe HJ and Barnett GO. Understanding and using the Medical Subject Headings (MeSH) vocabulary to perform literature searches. *JAMA* 1994 Apr 13; 271 (14) : 1103-1108.

McDonald SJ, Lefebvre C and Clarke M.J. Identifying reports of controlled trials in the *BMJ* and the *Lancet. British Medical Journal* 1996 Nov 2; 313 (7065) : 1116-1117.

McKibbon KA and Walker CJ. Panning for applied clinical research gold. *Online* 1993 Jul; 105-108.

McKibbon KA and Walker-Dilks C. *Evidence-based health care for librarians : panning for gold. How to apply research methodology to search for therapy, diagnosis, etiology, prognosis, review, and meta-analysis articles.* Ontario : Health Information Research Unit, McMaster University, 1995.

McKibbon KA, Wilczynski NL and Walker Dilks CJ. How to search for and find evidence about therapy. *Evidence Based Medicine* 1996; 1 (3) : 70-72.

Moore M. Battling the biomedical information explosion : a plan for implementing a quality filtered database. *Medical Reference Services Quarterly* 1989 Spring; 8 (1) : 13-19.

Muir Gray JA. Searching for evidence. In:- *Evidence-based health care : How to make health policy and management decisions,* by JA Muir Gray. London : Churchill Livingstone, 1997. 59-68.

Swanson DR. Medical literature as a potential source of new knowledge. *Bulletin of the Medical Library Association* 1990 Jan; 78 (1) 29-37.

Wilczynski NL, Walker CJ, McKibbon KA et al. Reasons for the loss of sensitivity and specificity of methodologic MeSH terms and textwords in MEDLINE. *Proceedings of the Annual Symposium on Computer Applications In Medical Care.* 1995 : 436-440.

Structured reporting

Froom P and Froom J. Deficiencies in structured medical abstracts. *Journal of Clinical Epidemiology* 1993 Jul; 46(7) : 591-595.

Harbourt AM, Knecht LS and Humphreys BL. Structured abstracts in MEDLINE, 1989-1991. *Bulletin of the Medical Library Association* 1995 Apr; 83(2) : 190-195.

Haynes RB, Mulrow CD, Huth EJ et al. More informative abstracts revisited. *Annals of Internal Medicine* 1990; 113(1) : 69-76.

Rennie D. Reporting randomized controlled trials : an experiment and a call for responses from readers. *JAMA* 1994; 273 (13) : 1054-1055.

Taddio A, Pain T, Fassos FF et al. Quality of nonstructured and structured abstracts of original research articles in the British Medical Journal, the Canadian Medical Association

Journal and the Journal of the American Medical Association. *Canadian Medical Association Journal* 1994 May 15; 150(10) : 1611-1615.

The Structured Reporting of Trials Group. A proposal for structured reporting of randomized controlled trials. *JAMA* 1994; 272 (24) : 1926-1931.

Wilczynski NL; Walker-CJ; McKibbon-KA et al. Preliminary assessment of the effect of more informative (structured) abstracts on citation retrieval from MEDLINE. *Medinfo* 1995; 8 Pt 2 : 1457-61.

Wofford JL, Moran WP, Wilson MC et al. Are abstracts alone useful enough to guide evidence based clinical decisions? *Journal of General Internal Medicine* 1995; 10 (4 Suppl) : 50.

INFORMATICS

Booth A. In search of the evidence : informing effective practice. *Journal of Clinical Effectiveness* 1996; 1 (1) : 25-29.

Booth A. Teaching evidence-based medicine - lessons for information professionals. *IFMH Inform* 1995 Summer; 6 (2) : 5-6.

Booth A, Ford N, Miller D et al. Towards machine support for evidence based information seeking. In : Lloyd-Williams M (ed). *SHIMR 96 : Proceedings of the Second International Symposium on Health Information Management Research.* University of Sheffield, 27-29 March, 1996. Sheffield : Centre for Health Information Management Research, University of Sheffield, 1996.

Coiera E. Evidence Based Medicine, the Internet and the rise of Medical Informatics. *Hewlett Packard Laboratories Technical Report*, 1996, No. 26. Available on the World Wide Web at:-
http://www-uk.hpl.hp.com/people/ewc/papers/orgyn/orgyn.htm

Haines M. Librarians and Evidence-based purchasing. *Evidence-Based Purchasing* 1995 June; (8) : 1,4

Haynes RB, Hayward RSA, Jadad A et al. Evidence based health informatics : an overview of the Health Information Research Unit at McMaster University. *Leadership in Health Services* 1996 May/June; 5 (3) : 41-44.

Haynes RB; Hayward RS and Lomas-J Bridges between health care research evidence and clinical practice. *Journal of the American Medical Informatics Association* 1995 Nov-Dec; 2(6) : 342-350. Also available as *Bridges between Evidence and Practice.* on the Internet at :
http://hiru.mcmaster.ca/ebm/informat/bridges.htm

Hayward RS, Hogeterp JA, Langton KB et al. GAP : a computer-assisted design tool for the development and analysis of evidence-based automated questionnaires. *Medinfo.* 1995; 8 Pt 2 : 934-937.

Lowry F. Computers a cornerstone of evidence-based care, conference told. *Canadian-Medical Association Journal.* 1995 Dec 1; 153(11) : 1636-9

McCarthy LH. Evidence-based medicine : an opportunity for health sciences librarians. *Medical Reference Services Quarterly* 1996; 15 (4) : 63.

Mead TL and Richards DT. Librarian participation in meta-analysis projects. *Bulletin of the Medical Library Association* 1995 Oct; 83 (4) : 461-464.

Needham G. A GRiPPing yarn - getting research into practice : a case study. *Health Libraries Review* 1994; 11 (4) : 269-277.

Palmer J. Finding the evidence. *Health Libraries Review* 1994; 11 (4) : 282-286

Palmer J. Yet more evidence.....changing professional practice. *Health Libraries Review* 1996; 13 : 121-123.

Phillips KA and Bero LA. Improving the use of information in medical effectiveness research. *International Journal for Quality in Healthcare* 1996 Feb; 8 (1) : 21-30.

Presley F. The need for evidence based medicine. *Assignation* 1996; 13 (2) : 41

Schell CL and Rathe R J. Meta-analysis : a tool for medical and scientific discoveries. *Bulletin of the Medical Library Association* 1992; 80 (3) : 219-222.

Sim I and Rennels G. A trial bank model for the publication of clinical trials. *Proceedings of the Annual Symposium on Computer Applications in Medical Care.* 1995 : 863-867.

CRITICAL APPRAISAL

User Guides to the Medical Literature (JAMA)

Guyatt G, Rennie D and the Evidence Based Medicine Working Group. Why Users' Guides? EBM Working Paper Series #1. Only available on the Internet as : *http://HIRU.MCMASTER.CA/ebm/userguid/0_users.htm*.

Guyatt GH. Users' guides to the medical literature. *JAMA* 1993; 270 (17) : 2096-2097.

Oxman A, Sackett, DL & Guyatt GH. Users' guides to the medical literature. I. How to get started. JAMA 1993 Nov 3; 270 (17) : 2093-2095. Also available on the Internet as : *http://HIRU.MCMASTER.CA/ebm/userguid/1_intro.htm*.

Guyatt GH, Sackett DL and Cook DJ. Users' guides to the medical literature. II. How to use an article about therapy or prevention. A. Are the results of the study valid? *JAMA* 1993; 270 2598-2601.

Guyatt GH, Sackett DL and Cook DJ. Users' guides to the medical literature. II. How to use an article about therapy or prevention. B. What were the results and will they help me in caring for my patients? *JAMA* 1994; 271:59-63. Available on the Internet as : *http://HIRU.MCMASTER.CA/ebm/userguid/2_tx.htm*.

Jaeschke R, Guyatt G and Sackett DL. Users' guides to the medical literature. III. How to use an article about a diagnostic test. A. Are the results of the study valid? *JAMA* 1994 Feb 2; 271 (5) : 389-391.

Jaeschke R, Gordon H, Guyatt G & Sackett DL. Users' guides to the medical literature. III. How to use an article about a diagnostic test. B. what are the results and will they help me in caring for my patients? *JAMA* 1994; 271 : 703-707. Available on the Internet as : *http://HIRU.MCMASTER.CA/ebm/userguid/3_dx.htm*.

Levine M, Walter S, Lee H, Haines T, Holbrook A & Moyer V.. Users'guides to the medical literature. IV. How to use an article about harm. *JAMA* 1994 May 25; 271 (20) 1615-1619. available on the Internet as : *http://HIRU.MCMASTER.CA/ebm/userguid/4_harm.htm*.

Laupacis A, Wells G, Richardson S & Tugwell P. Users' guides to the medical literature. V. How to use an article about prognosis. *JAMA* 1994; 272 : 234-237. Available on the Internet as : *http://HIRU.MCMASTER.CA/ebm/userguid/5_prog.htm*.

Oxman AD, Cook DJ, Guyatt GH. Users' guides to the medical literature. VI. How to use an overview. *JAMA* 1994; 272 (17) : 1367-1371. available on the Internet as : *http://HIRU.MCMASTER.CA/ebm/userguid/6_over.htm*.

Richardson WS , Detsky AS. Users' guides to the medical literature. VII. How to use a Clinical Decision Analysis. A. Are the results of the study valid? *JAMA* 1995; 273 (16) : 1292-1295.

Richardson WS, Detsky AS. Users' guides to the medical literature. VII. How to use a Clinical Decision Analysis. B. What are the results and will they help me in caring for my patients? *JAMA* 1995; 273 (20) : 1610-1613. available on the Internet as : *http://HIRU.MCMASTER.CA/ebm/userguid/7_da.htm.*

Hayward RSA, Wilson MC, Tunis SR, Bass EB, Guyatt G. Users' guides to the medical literature. VIII. How to use clinical practice guidelines. A. Are the recommendations valid? *JAMA* 1995; 274 (7) : 570-574.

Wilson MC, Hayward RSA, Tunis SR, Bass EB, Guyatt G. Users' guides to the medical literature. VIII. How to use clinical practice guidelines B. What are the recommendations and will they help you in caring for your patients? *JAMA* 1995 Nov 22-29; 274 (20) : 1630-1632. Available on the Internet as : *http://HIRU.MCMASTER.CA/ebm/userguid/8_cpg.htm.*

Guyatt GH, Sackett DL, Sinclair JC et al. Users' Guides to the medical literature. IX. A Method for Grading Health Care Recommendations. *JAMA* 1995 Dec 13; 274 (22) : 1800-1804.

Naylor CD and Guyatt GH Users guides to the medical literature. X. How to use an article reporting variations in the outcomes of health services. Evidence-Based Medicine Working Group. *JAMA.* 1996 Feb 21; 275(7) : 554-558. available on the Internet as : *http://HIRU.MCMASTER.CA/ebm/userguid/10_hsr.htm.*

Naylor CD and Guyatt GH. Users' guides to the medical literature. XI. How to use an article about a clinical utilization review. Evidence-Based Medicine Working Group. *JAMA.* 1996 May 8; 275 (18) : 1435-1439. Available on the Internet as :
http://HIRU.MCMASTER.CA/ebm/userguid/9_econ.htm.

Guyatt GH, Naylor CD, Juniper E et al. Users' guides to the medical literature. XII. How to use articles about health-related quality of life. Evidence-Based Medicine Working Group. *JAMA* 1997 Apr 16; 277 (15) : 1232-1237.

Teaching Critical Appraisal

Abyad A. Debate journal club teaches critical appraisal skills. *Family Medicine* 1995; 27 (4) : 226.

Bennett KJ, Sackett DL and Haynes RB et al. A controlled trial of teaching critical appraisal of the clinical literature to medical students. *JAMA* 1987; 257 : 2451-2454.

Burls A and Milne R. Evaluating the evidence : an introduction. *Journal of Clinical Effectiveness* 1996; 1 (2) : 59-62.

Domholdt E, Flaherty JL and Phillips JM. Critical appraisal of research literature by expert and inexperienced physical therapy therapy researchers. *Physical Therapy* 1994 Sep; 74 (9) : 853-840.

Dorsch JL, Frasca MA and Wilson ML et al. A multidisciplinary approach to information and critical appraisal. *Bulletin of the Medical Library Association* 1990 Jan; 78 (1) : 38-44.

Ebell M. Teaching critical appraisal of the literature : an introduction to the *JFP* Journal Club. *Journal of Family Practice* 1994; 38 : 457-458.

Frasca MA, Dorsch JL, Aldag JC et al. A multidisciplinary approach to information management and critical appraisal instruction : a controlled study. *Bulletin of the Medical Library Association* 1992 Jan; 80 (1) : 23-28.

Heiligman F. Resident evaluation of a family practice residency journal club. *Family Medicine* 1991; 23 : 152-153.

Hicks C. Bridging the gap between research and practice : an assessment of the value of a study day in developing critical research reading skills in midwives. *Midwifery* 1994; 10 : 18-25.

Jamison JR. Innovations in teaching : a learning format designed to enhance critical appraisal skills. *Journal- Canadian Chiropractic Association* 1995; 39 (4) : 217

Konen JC and Fromm BS. A family practice residency curriculum in critical appraisal of the Medical Literature. *Family Medicine* 1990 Jul-Aug; 22 (4) : 284-287.

Langkamp DL. The effect of a medical journal club on residents' knowledge of clinical epidemiology and biostatistics. *Family Medicine* 1992; 24 : 528-530.

Lee HN, Sauve JS, Farkouh ME, Sackett DL. The critically appaised topic : a standardised aid for the presentation and storage of evidence-based medicine.*Clinical Research* 1993; 41 : 543A.

Linzer M, Brown JT, Frazier LM et al. Impact of a medical journal club on house-staff reading habits, knowledge and critical appraisal skills : a randomized control trial. *JAMA* 1988; 260 (17) : 2537-2541.

MacAuley D. Critical reading using the R.E.A.D.E.R. acronym at an international workshop. *Family Practice* 1996; 13 (1) : 104-105.

Milne R & Chambers L. How to read a research article critically. *Health Libraries Review* 1993; 10 : 39.

Milne R, Donald A and Chambers L. Piloting short workshops on the critical appraisal of reviews. *Health Trends* 1995; 27(4):120

Milne R and Oliver S. Evidence-based consumer health information : developing teaching in critical appraisal skills. *International Journal for Quality in Health Care* 1996; 8 (5) : 439.

Moberg-Wolff EA and Kosahih JB. Journal clubs : prevalence, format and efficacy in PM&R. *American Journal of Physical Medicine and Rehabilitation* 1995; 74 : 224-229.

Riegelman RK. Effects of teaching first-year medical students skills to read medical literature. *Journal of Medical Education* 1986 Jun; 61 : 454-460.

Seelig CB. Affecting resident's literature reading attitudes, behaviors and knowledge through a journal club intervention. *Journal of General Internal Medicine* 1991; 6 : 330-334.

Shin JH, Haynes RB and Johnson ME. Effect of problem based, self directed undergraduate education on life-long learning. *Canadian Medical Association Journal* 1993; 148 (6) : 969-976.

Sidorov J. How are Internal Medicine Residency Journal Clubs organized and what makes them successful? *Archives of Internal Medicine* 1995; 155 : 1193-1197.

Tibbles L and Sanford R. The research journal club : a mechanism for research utilization. *Clinical Nurse Specialist* 1994 Jan; 8 (1) : 23-26.

Woods JR and Winkel CE. Journal Club format emphasizing techniques of critical reading. *Journal of Medical Education* 1982; 57 : 799-801.

Other items

Avis M. Reading research critically : an introduction to appraisal : designs and objectives.....Part 1. *Journal of Clinical Nursing* 1994 Jul; 3 (4) : 227-234.

Avis M. Reading research critically : an introduction to appraisal : assessing the evidence.....Part 2. *Journal of Clinical Nursing* 1994 Sep; 3 (5) : 271-277.

Cluzeau F et al. Towards valid clinical guidelines : development of a critical appraisal instrument. *Health Care Risk Report* 1996 Feb; 2 (3) : 16-18.

Drummond A. Reviewing a research article. *British Journal of Occupational Therapy* 1996; 59 (2) : 84-86.

Fowkes FGR and Fulton PM. Critical appraisal of published research : introductory guidelines. *British Medical Journal* 1991; 302:1136-40.

Hek G. Guidelines on conducting a critical research evaluation. *Nursing Standard* 1996 Oct 30; 11 (6) : 40-43.

Hutchinson BG. Critical appraisal of review articles. *Canadian Family Physician* 1993; 39 : 1097-102.

Jones R and Kinmouth AL. *Critical Reading for primary care.* Oxford : Oxford University Press, 1995.

Katz RT et al. Critical evaluation of clinical research. *Archives of Physical Medicine and Rehabilitation* 1995; 76 (1) : 82-93.

Medicines Resource Centre. An introduction to assessing medical literature. *MeReC Briefing* 1995 Feb; (9) : 1-8. (Published by Medicines Resource Centre, Hamilton House, 24 Pall Mall, LIVERPOOL, L3 6AL. Tel : 0151 231 6044, Fax : 0151 236 2039)

Muir Gray JA. Appraising the quality of research. In:- *Evidence-based health care : how to make health policy and management decisions*, by JA Muir Gray. London : Churchill Livingstone, 1997. 69-102.

Nony P, Cucherat M, Haugh MC et al. Critical reading of the meta-analysis of clinical trials. *Therapie* 1995 Jul-Aug; 50 (4) : 339-351.

Patrick SC. Critical appraisal of the medical literature : selected readings. *Medical Reference Services Quarterly* 1994 Fall; 13 (3) : 37-58.

Sheldon TA, Song F, Davey Smith G. Critical appraisal of the medical literature : how to assess whether health-care interventions do more good than harm. In : Drummond MF, Maynard A. *Purchasing and providing cost-effective health care*. Edinburgh : Churchill Livingstone, 1993 : 31-48.

Thomas C. Critical appraisal of literature. In:- *Research methods in primary care*, edited by Y Carter and C Thomas. Oxford : Radcliffe Medical Press, 1997.

SYSTEMATIC REVIEWS

British Medical Journal Series on Systematic Reviews

Chalmers, I. & Altman, DG. (eds) *Systematic reviews.* London : British Medical Journal Publishing, 1995. This book contains revised versions of some, but not all, of the following papers:-

Haynes RB. [editorial] . Clinical review articles. *British Medical Journal* 1992; 309 : 330-331.

Mulrow CD. Rationale for systematic reviews. *British Medical Journal* 1994; 309 : 597-599.

Oxman AD. Checklists for review articles. *British Medical Journal* 1994; 309 : 648-651.

Knipschild P. Some examples. *British Medical Journal* 1994; 309 : 719-721.

Eysenck HJ. Meta-analysis and its problems. *British Medical Journal* 1994; 309 : 789-792.

Chalmers I. & Haynes B. Reporting, updating and correcting systematic reviews of the effects of health care. *British Medical Journal* 1994; 309 : 862-865.

Clarke MJ. & Stewart LA. Obtaining data from randomised controlled trials : how much do we need for reliable and informative meta-analyses? *British Medical Journal* 1994; 309 : 1007-1010.

Managing the review process

Cooper HM. *Integrative Research : A Guide for Literature Reviews.* 2nd ed. Newbury Park, CA : Sage Publications, 1989.

Cooper HM. *The Integrative Research Review : A systematic approach.* Beverly Hills, CA. Sage Publications, 1984.

Cullum N. Critical reviews of the literature. In : Hardey M & Mulhall A (eds.) *Nursing research : theory and practice.* London : Chapman & Hall, 1994 : 43-57.

Droogan J and Song F. The process and importance of systematic reviews. *Nurse Researcher* 1996 Sep; 4 (1) : 15-26.

Enkin M and Hetherington J. Collecting the evidence systematically - ensuring that it is complete and up-to-date. *International Journal of Technology Assessment In Health Care,* 1996; 12 (2) : 276-279.

Goodman C. *Literature Searching and evidence interpretation for assessing health care practices.* Stockholm : SBU (Swedish Council on Technology Assessment in Health Care), 1993.

Long AF and Sheldon TA. Enhanced effective and acceptable purchaser decisions : overview and methods. *Quality in Health Care* 1992; 1 : 74-76.

Muir Gray JA. Two classes of creativity - Improving systematic reviews. *Journal of Epidemiology and Community Health* 1994; 48 : 4-5.

NHS Centre for Reviews and Dissemination. *Undertaking systematic reviews of research on effectiveness : CRD Guidelines for those carrying out or commissioning reviews.* (CRD Report 4), York : University of York, 1996.

NHS Centre for Reviews and Dissemination. *Information Sheet 5 : Systematic Review Guidelines Summary.* York : University of York, n.d.

Ohlsson A. Systematic reviews - theory and practice. *Scandinavian Journal of Clinical and Laboratory Investigation, Supplement* 1994; 54 : 25-32.

Oxman A, Guyatt GH. The science of reviewing research. *Annals of the New York Academy of Sciences* 1993; 703 : 125-134.

Oxman AD. *Preparing and maintaining systematic reviews : the Cochrane Collaboration Handbook.* Oxford, Cochrane Collaboration. 1994.

Power NR, Turner JA, Maklan CW & Ersek M. Alternative methods for formal literature review and meta-analysis in AHCPR Patient Outcomes Research Teams. *Medical Care* 1994; 32 (7) Suppl : JS22-JS37.

Smith JT, Smith MC and Stullenbarger E. Decision points in the integrative research review process : a flow-chart approach. *Medical Reference Services Quarterly* 1991; 10 (2) : 47-72

Smith JT, Smith MC, Stullenbarger E et al. Integrative review and meta-analysis : an application. *Medical Reference Services Quarterly* 1994; 13 (1) : 57-72

Other items

Cook DJ, Mulrow CD and Haynes RB. Systematic reviews: synthesis of best evidence for clinical decisions. *Annals of Internal Medicine* 1997 Mar 1; 126 : 364-371.

Dickson R and Cullum N. Systematic reviews : how to use the clinical evidence. *Nursing Standard* 1996; 10 (20) : 32.

Dickson R and Entwistle V. Systematic reviews : keeping up with research evidence. *Nursing Standard* 1996; 10 (19) : 32

Duley L. Systematic Reviews - What can they do for you? *Journal of the Royal Society of Medicine,* 1996, 89 (5) : 242-244.

Franklin J. Systematic reviews. *Journal of the Royal Society of Medicine* 1996; 89 (9)

Hughes EG. Systematic literature review and metaanalysis. *Seminars in Reproductive Endocrinology* 1996; 14 (2) : 161-169

Lancaster T. Systematic reviews and meta-analysis. In:- *Research methods in primary care,* edited by Y Carter and C Thomas. Oxford : Radcliffe Medical Press, 1997.

Mulrow CD. The medical review article : state of the science. *Annals of Internal Medicine* 1987; 106 (3) : 485-488.

NHS Centre for Reviews and Dissemination. *Information Sheet 7 : Bibliography on conducting and using systematic reviews* . York : University of York, n.d.

Oh VMS. Systematic reviews of randomised intervention trials : Better tools for Doctors? . *Annals- Academy of Medicine Singapore* 1996; 25 (4) : 485

Rosenfeld RM. How to systematically review the medical literature. *Otolaryngology-Head And Neck Surgery* 1996, 115 (1) : 53-63.

Systematic search offers a sound evidence. *Nursing Times* 1996 Jan 24; 92 (4) : 37-39.

COCHRANE COLLABORATION

Alvarez Dardet C, Ruiz MT. Thomas McKeown and Archibald Cochrane : A journey through the diffusion of their ideas. *British Medical Journal* 1993; 306:1252-1255.

Anon. Cochrane's legacy [editorial] . *Lancet* 1992; 340 : 1131-1132.

Bero L, Rennie O. The Cochrane Collaboration : preparing, maintaining, and disseminating systematic reviews of the effects of health care. *Journal - American Medical Association.* 1995 Dec 27; 274 (24) : 1935-1938.

Boissel JP and Haugh M. Cochrane Collaboration for treatment information. *Presse Medicale* 1996; 25 (23) : 1047-1048.

Chalmers I. What would Archie Cochrane have said? *Lancet* 1995; 346 (8985) : 1300

Chalmers I, Sandercock P, Wennberg J. The Cochrane Collaboration : Preparing, maintaining, and disseminating systematic reviews of the effects of health care. *Annals of the New York Academy of Sciences* 1993; 703:156-165.

Chalmers I, Dickersin K, Chalmers TC. Getting to grips with Archie Cochrane's agenda. *British Medical Journal* 1994; 305:786-8.

Chalmers I, Enkin M and Keirse MJNC. Preparing and updating systematic reviews of randomized controlled trials of health care. *Milbank Quarterly* 1993; 71 (3) : 411-37.

Cochrane AL. *Effectiveness and efficiency. Random reflections on health services.* London : Nuffield Provincial Hospitals Trust, 1972.

Cochrane AL. 1931-1971 : a critical review, with particular reference to the medical profession. In : *Medicines for the year 2000.* London : Office of Health Economics, 1979.

The Cochrane Collaboration. *Introductory brochure.* Oxford : Cochrane Collaboration, 1993.

Enkin M and Hetherington J. Collecting the evidence systematically : ensuring that it is complete and up-to-date. *International Journal of Technology Assessment in Health Care* 1996; 12 (2) : 276-279.

Freemantle N, Grilli R, Grimshaw J et al. Implementing findings of medical research : the Cochrane Collaboration on Effective Professional Practice. *Quality in Health Care* 1995; 4 : 45-47.

Fullerton-Smith I. How members of the Cochrane Collaboration prepare and maintain systematic reviews of the effects of health care. *Evidence-Based Medicine* 1995; 1 (1) : 7-8

Godlee F. The Cochrane Collaboration - deserves the support of doctors and governments. *British Medical Journal* 1994; 309:969-970.

Greenhalgh T. The Cochrane Collaboration : Do you have the CD ROM for the Cochrane Controlled Trials Register? *Pharmaceutical Times -London* 1996 Jul; 23

Haugh MC, Boissel JP, Pignon JP et al. The Cochrane Collaboration - the need for international co-operation. *Therapie* 1996; 51 (3) : 253-256

Herxheimer A. The Cochrane Collaboration : making the results of controlled trials properly accessible. *Postgraduate Medical Journal* 1993; 69 : 867-8.

Herxheimer A : The Cochrane Collaboration. Making the results of controlled trials properly accessible. *International Journal of Risk and Safety in Medicine* 1994; 4:241-244.

Huston P. Cochrane Collaboration helping unravel tangled web woven by international research. *Canadian Medical Association Journal* 1996; 154 (9) : 1389

Jones A : Second International Cochrane Colloquium - Official Annual Meeting of the Cochrane Collaboration : a conference report. *Respiratory Care* 1995;40:171-174.

Lefebvre C. The Cochrane Collaboration : ensuring quality in reviews of the effects of health care. *Inform* 1994 December; 4-5.

Lefebvre C. The Cochrane Collaboration : the role of the UK Cochrane Centre in identifying the evidence. *Health Libraries Review* 1994; 11 : 235-242

McPherson K. The best and the enemy of the good : randomised controlled trials, uncertainty, and assessing the role of patient choice in medical decision making (The Cochrane Lecture). *Journal of Epidemiology and Community Health* 1994; 48 (1) : 6-15.

Milne R and Thorogood M. Hand searching the *Journal of Epidemiology and Community Health* as part of the Cochrane Collaboration. *Journal of Epidemiology and Community Health* 1996 Apr; 50 (2) : 178-181.

Milne R and Mead J. The Cochrane Collaboration and clinical audit. *Medical Audit News* 1993; 3 (5) : 73-74.

Neal B, Rodgers A, Mackie MJ et al. 40 Years of randomized trials in the *New Zealand Medical Journal*. *New Zealand Medical Journal* 1996, 109 (1031) : 372-373.

Orleans M. Meta-analysis and the Cochrane Centers. *Public Health Reports- US* 1995; 110 (5) : 633.

Paterson-Brown S, Fisk NM and Wyatt JC. Uptake of meta-analytical overviews of effective care in English obstetric units. *British Journal of Obstetrics and Gynaecology*, 1995; 102 (4) : 297-301.

Paterson-Brown S, Wyatt JC, Fisk NM. Are clinicians interested in up to date reviews of effective care? *British Medical Journal* 1993; 307 (6917) : 1464.

Pignon JP. Interest of the Cochrane Collaboration - the point of view of a metaanalysis practitioner. *Therapie* 1996; 51 (3) : 257-260.

Ramirez G. Evidence-based medicine : the Cochrane Collaboration [editorial] *Hosp-Pract-Off-Ed.* 1996 Apr 15; 31(4) : 11-4

Robinson A. Research, practice and the Cochrane Collaboration. *Canadian Medical Association Journal* 1995; 152(6):883-889.

Sackett D. The Cochrane Collaboration. *ACP Journal Club*; 1994 May-Jun : A11. (*Ann Intern Med 120, suppl 3*).

Sackett DL. Cochrane Collaboration. *British Medical Journal* 1994;309 (6967):1514-1515.

Savage I. Broad Spectrum : keeping up with Cochrane. *Pharmaceutical Journal.* 1995 Nov 18; 255 (6867) : 676.

Sheldon T & Chalmers I. The UK Cochrane Centre and the NHS Centre for Reviews and Dissemination : respective roles within the Information Systems Strategy of the NHS R&D Programme, co-ordination and principles underlying collaboration. *Health Economics* 1994; 3 : 201-203.

Stewart LA and Clarke MJ. Practical methodology of meta-analyses (overviews) using updated individual patient data. Cochrane Working Group. *Statistics in Medicine* 1995 Oct 15; 14(19) : 2057-79

Tsutani K. The Cochrane Collaboration - What is the Cochrane Collaboration? *Family Practice* 1996; 13 (5) : R 4-R 5

Cochrane Collaboration and Specialties

Alternative Medicine

White A. The Cochrane Collaboration, Medline and *Acupuncture in Medicine. Acupuncture in Medicine* 1995; 13 (2) : 66

Audit

Lancaster T and Silagy C. The Cochrane Database of Systematic Reviews : a resource for evidence-based standard setting in clinical audit. *Audit Trends* 1996 Mar; 4 (1) : 26-27.

Gastroenterology

McDonald JWD. The Cochrane Collaboration Inflammatory Bowel Disease Collaborative Review Group. *Canadian Journal of Gastroenterology* 1995; 9:241

McDonald JWD, Sutherland LR. The Cochrane-Collaboration IBD Review Group. *Inflammatory Bowel Diseases* 1996; 2 (2) : 115-117.

Geriatrics

Barer D. Narrative or systematic reviews : can we be more 'evidence-based'? *Reviews in Clinical Gerontology* 1995; 5 (4) : 365

Dickinson E, Rochon P : Cochrane collaboration in health care of elderly people. *Age and Ageing* 1995 Jul;24:265-266.

Neurology

Counsel CE, Fraser H and Sandercock PAG. Archie Cochrane's challenge : Can periodically updated reviews of all randomised controlled trials relevant to neurology and neurosurgery be produced? *Journal of Neurology Neurosurgery and Psychiatry* 1994;57:529-533.

Marson A, Beghi E, Berg A et al. The Cochrane Collaboration - Systematic Reviews And their relevance to epilepsy. *Epilepsia* 1996; 37 (10) : 917-921.

Obstetrics and Gynaecology

Enkin MW : Systematic summaries and dissemination of evidence : The Cochrane pregnancy and childbirth database. *Seminars in Perinatology* 1995;19:155-160.

Farquhar CM. The need for systematic reviews in the treatment of menstrual disorders-another Cochrane collaborative review group is born. *British Journal of Obstetrics and Gynaecology* 1996; 103 (6) : 497-500

Hyde C : Who uses the Cochrane Pregnancy and Childbirth Database? *British Medical Journal* 1995; 310:1140-1141.

Sakala C. The Cochrane Pregnancy and Childbirth Database : implications for perinatal care policy and practice in the United States. *Evaluation and the Health Professions* 1995; 18 (4) : 428.

Oral Health

Shaw WC. The Cochrane Collaboration : Oral Health Group. *British Dental Journal* 1994; 177 : 272-273

Pharmacology

Herxheimer A. Systematic reviews of randomised controlled trials : Important for clinical pharmacologists. *British Journal of Clinical Pharmacology* 1993;36 : 507-509.

Herxheimer A. Systematic reviews of RCTs : How pharmaceutical physicians and their colleagues can contribute. *Pharmaceutical Medicine* 1994;8 : 43-48.

Physiotherapy

Newham D. The Cochrane Collaboration. What is it, how does it work, and what has it to do with physiotherapy? *Physiotherapy* 1995;81:405-407.

Primary Health Care

Silagy C. Developing a register of randomised controlled trials in primary care. *British Medical Journal* 1993; 306 : 897-900.

Silagy CA and Jewell D. Review of 39 years of randomized controlled trials in the *British Journal of General Practice. British Journal of General Practice* 1994; 44 : 359-363

Silagy C and Lancaster T. The Cochrane Collaboration in Primary Health Care. *Family Practice* 1993; 10 : 364-365.

Wise P and Drury M. Pharmaceutical trials in general practice : the first 100 protocols. An audit by the clinical research ethics committee of the Royal College of General Practitioners. *British Medical Journal* 1996; Nov 16; 313 (7067) : 1245-1248

Psychiatry

Adams C, Anderson J, Awad G, et al : Schizophrenia and The Cochrane Collaboration. *Schizophrenia Research* 1994;13:185-187.

Adams CE. A systematic approach to evaluation of care : the Cochrane Collaboration. *Journal of Psychosomatic Research* 1995; 39 (8) : 927.

White P. Identification of Randomized Clinical-Trials in the *Australian and New Zealand Journal of Psychiatry* for the Cochrane Collaboration . *Australian and New Zealand Journal of Psychiatry* 1996; 30 (4) : 531-533.

Public Health

Milne R and Thorogood M. Hand searching the *Journal of Community Health* as part of the Cochrane Collaboration. *Journal of Epidemiology and Community Health* 1996; 50 (2), 178-181

Respiratory Medicine

Donald PR : Proposed Cochrane Collaboration for tuberculosis treatment. *South African Medical Journal* 1994;84:507

Rheumatology

Brooks P and Kirwan JR : Evidence-based medical practice : The Cochrane collaboration and osteoarthritis. *British Journal of Rheumatology* 1995; 34:403-404.

Sports Medicine

Hart LE and Meeuwisse WH. Systematic reviews come of age : the Cochrane Collaboration [editorial] . *Clinical Journal of Sport Medicine* 1996; 6 (1) : 63

Stroke

Counsell C, Warlow C, Sandercock P, et al : The Cochrane Collaboration Stroke Review Group : Meeting the need for systematic reviews in stroke care. *Stroke* 1995;26:498-502.

Surgery

Bradbury AW, Ruckley CV. Variations in Vascular Practice and the Cochrane Collaboration. *European Journal of Vascular and Endovascular Surgery* 1996; 11 (2) : 125

META-ANALYSIS

Anonymous. Systematic overview of controlled trials (meta-analysis) helps clarify treatment effects. *Drug and Therapeutics Bulletin* 1992;30:25-27.

Antman EM, Lau J, Kupelnick B, Mosteller F & Chalmers TC. A comparison of results of meta-analyses of randomized controlled trials and recommendations of clinical experts. Treatments for myocardial infarction. *JAMA* 1992; 268 : 240-248.

Berkey CS, Anderson JJ and Hoaglin DC. Multiple-outcome meta-analysis of clinical trials. *Statistics in Medicine.* 1996 Mar 15; 15(5) : 537-57

Boden WE. Meta-analysis in clinical trials reporting : has a tool become a weapon? *American Journal of Cardiology* 1992; 69 : 681-686.

Borzak S; Ridker PM. Discordance between meta-analyses and large-scale randomized, controlled trials. Examples from the management of acute myocardial infarction. *Annals of Internal Medicine.* 1995 Dec 1; 123(11) : 873-7

Cappelleri JC, Ioannidis JPA, Schmid CH. et al. Large trials vs meta-analysis of smaller trials : how do their results compare? *JAMA* 1996 Oct 23-30; 276 (16) : 1332-1338.

Charlton BG. The uses and abuses of metaanalysis. *Family Practice*, 1996; 13 (4) : 397-401.

Charlton BG. Practice guidelines and practical judgement : the role of mega-trials, meta-analysis and consensus. *British Journal of General Practice* 1994; 44 : 290-1

Clarke MJ and Stewart LA. Obtaining data from randomised controlled trials : how much do we need reliable and informative meta-analyses? *British Medical Journal* 1994; 309 : 1007-10.

Clarke MJ and Stewart LA. Systematic reviews of randomized controlled trials : the need for complete data. *Journal of Evaluation in Clinical Practice* 1995; 1 (2) : 119-126.

Cook D. 'Cumulative meta analysis of clinical trials builds evidence for exemplary medical care' : Discussion. *Journal of Clinical Epidemiology* 1995;48:59-60.

Cook DJ, Guyatt GH, Ryan G et al. Should unpublished data be included in meta-analyses? Current convictions and controversies. *JAMA* 1993; 269 : 2749-2753.

Cook DJ, Sackett DL and Spitzer WO. Methodologic guidelines for systematic reviews of randomized control trials in health care from the Potsdam Consultation on meta-analysis. *Journal of Clinical Epidemiology* 1995; 48:167-171.

Cooper H and Hedges LV. *The Handbook of Research Synthesis.* New York : Russell Sage Foundation, 1994.

Correspondence Misleading meta-analysis. *BMJ.* 1995 Nov 11; 311(7015) : 1303-4 (One incorrect meta-analysis does not invalidate them all - Law-MR; Wald-NJ <u>and</u> Subject to many potential biases - Gilbody-S; House-A; Song-F et al, pp. 1303-1304).

D'Agostino RB and Weintraub M. Meta-analysis : a method for synthesizing research. *Clin Pharmacol-Ther.* 1995 Dec; 58(6) : 605-16

Detsky AS, Naylor CD, O'Rourke K et al. Incorporating variations in the quality of individual randomized controlled trials into meta-analysis. *Journal of Clinical Epidemiology* 1992; 45:255-265.

Dickersin K and Berlin J. Meta-analysis : state of the science. *Epidemiological Reviews.* 1992; 14:154-76.

Egger M and Davey Smith G. Misleading meta-analysis. *British Medical Journal* 1995; 310; 752-754.

Egger M, Davey-Smith G, Song F et al. Making sense of meta-analysis. *Pharmacoepidemiology and Drug Safety* 1993; 2 : 65-72.

Eysenck HJ. Meta-analysis and its problems. *British Medical Journal* 1994; 309 : 789-92.

Eysenck HJ. Meta-analysis or best-evidence synthesis? *Journal of Evaluation in Clinical Practice* 1995; 1 (1) : 29-36.

Feinstein AR. Meta-analysis : statistical alchemy for the 21st century *Journal of Clinical Epidemiology* 1995; 48 (1) : 71-80. [Discussion:- Liberati A, p. 81].

Finney DJ. A statistician looks at meta-analysis. *Journal of Clinical Epidemiology* 1995; 48 (1) : 87-104. [Discussion by Irwig L, p. 105].

Friedman HP and Goldberg JD. Meta-analysis : an introduction and point of view. *Hepatology.* 1996 Apr; 23(4) : 917-28

Greener J and Grimshaw J. Using meta-analysis to summarise evidence within systematic reviews. *Nurse Researcher* 1996 Sep; 4 (1) : 27-38.

Haines SJ and Walters BC. What is metaanalysis? *Surgical Neurology* 1995 Dec; 44 (6) : 581-582.

Hasselblad V et al. A survey of current problems in meta-analysis. *Medical Care* 1995; 33 (2) : 202-220.

Henderson WG, Moritz T; Goldman S et al. Use of cumulative meta-analysis in the design, monitoring, and final analysis of a clinical trial : a case study. *Controlled Clinical Trials.* 1995 Oct; 16(5) : 331-41.

Irwig L, Tosteson ANA, Gatsonis C et al. Guidelines for meta-analyses evaluating diagnostic tests. *Annals of Internal Medicine* 1994; 120:667-676

Lau J, Schmid CH and Chalmers TC. Cumulative meta-analysis of clinical trials builds evidence for exemplary medical care. *Journal of Clinical Epidemiology* 1995; 48 (1) : 45-58. [Discussion:- Cook D : 59]

Laupacis A. Research by collaboration (meta-analyses of individual patient data). *Lancet* 1995; 345 (8955) : 938.

Lee YJ. Conference on meta-analysis in the design and monitoring of clinical trials. *Statistics in Medicine* 1996; 15 (12) (Whole Issue).

Liberati A. 'Meta-analysis : Statistical alchemy for the 21st century' : Discussion. A plea for a more balanced view of meta-analysis and systematic overviews of the effect of health care interventions. *Journal of Clinical Epidemiology* 1995;48:81-86.

Light RJ. and Pillemer DB. *Summing up : the science of reviewing research.* Cambridge, MA : Harvard University Press, 1984.

Naylor CD. The case for failed meta-analyses. *Journal of Evaluation in Clinical Practice* 1995; 1 (1) :

Olsen J. Meta-analyses or collaborative studies. *Journal of Occupational and Environmental Medicine.* 1995 Aug; 37(8) : 897-902

Oxman AD and Guyatt GH. A consumer's guide to subgroup analysis. *Annals of Internal Medicine* 1992; 116 : 78-84.

Persaud-R. Misleading meta-analysis. "Fail safe N" is a useful mathematical measure of the stability of results [letter] . *BMJ* 1996 Jan 13; 312(7023) : 125

Pettiti DB. *Meta-analysis, decision analysis and cost-effectiveness analysis : methods for quantitative synthesis in medicine.* (Monographs in Epidemiology and Biostatistics, 24) Oxford : Oxford University Press, 1994.

Peto R. Why do we need systematic overviews of randomized trials? *Statistics in Medicine* 1987;6:233-240.

Prins JM and Buller HR. Meta-analysis : the final answer, or even more confusion? [letter] *Lancet* 1996 Jul 20; 348 (9021) : 199

Richards SM. Meta-analyses and overviews of randomised trials. *Blood Reviews.* 1995 Jun; 9 (2) : 85-91

Rosenthal R. *Meta-analytic Procedures for Social Research*, 2nd ed. Newbury Park, California: Sage, 1991.

Sacks HS, Berrier J, Reitman D et al. Meta-analyses of randomized controlled trials. *New England Journal of Medicine* 1987; 316 : 450-455.

Sacks HS, Reitman D, Pagano D et al. Meta-analysis : an update. *Mount Sinai Journal of Medicine* 1996 May-Sep; 63(3-4) : 216-24

Schmid JE. An overview of statistical issues and methods of meta-analysis. *Journal of Biopharmaceutical Statistics* 1991; 1 : 103-120.

Sharp SJ, Thompson SG and Altman DG. The relation between treatment benefit and underlying risk in meta-analysis. *BMJ* 1996 Sep 21; 313 (7059) : 735-738

Sim I and Hlatky MA. (1996) Growing pains of meta-analysis : advances in methodology will not remove the need for well designed trials. *BMJ* 1996 Sep 21; 313 (7059) : 702-703.

Slavin RE. Best evidence synthesis : an intelligent alternative to meta-analysis. *Journal of Clinical Epidemiology* 1995; 48 (1) : 9-18 [Discussion : Letzel H, p.19]

Smith TC, Spiegelhalter DJ and Thomas A. Bayesian approaches to random-effects meta-analysis : a comparative study. *Statistics in Medicine.* 1995 Dec 30; 14(24) : 2685-99

Spector TD and Thompson SG. Potential and limitations of meta-analysis. *Journal of Epidemiology and Community Health* 1991; 45 : 89-92.

Stewart LA and Parmar MKB. Meta-analysis of the literature or of individual patient data : is there a difference? *Lancet* 1993; 341 : 418-22.

Stram DO. Meta-analysis of published data using a linear mixed-effects model. *Biometrics.* 1996 Jun; 52(2) : 536 44

Thompson SG. Why sources of heterogeneity in meta-analysis should be investigated. *British Medical Journal* 1994; 309 : 1351-5.

Thompson SG and Pocock SJ. Can meta-analysis be trusted? *Lancet* 1991; 338 : 1127-30. [See also comments by Chalmers I. *Lancet* 1991; 338 : 1464-1465 (Letter) and Stewart LA et al. *Lancet* 1991; 338 : 1465 (Letter)].

Villar J, Carroli G and Belizan JM. Predictive ability of meta-analyses of randomised controlled trials. *Lancet* 1995; 345 : 772-776.

West RR. A look at the statistical overview (or meta-analysis). *Journal of the Royal College of Physicians London* 1993; 27 : 111-115.

Wolf FM. *Meta-analysis : quantitative methods for research synthesis.* Sage University Paper on quantitative applications in the Social Sciences, Series Number 07-059. Beverly Hills : Sage Publications, 1986.

Yusuf S, Wiftes J, Probstfield J et al. Analysis and interpretation of treatment effects in subgroups of patients in randomized clinical trials. *JAMA* 1991; 266 : 93-98.

SCALES, CHECKLISTS AND QUALITY OF STUDIES

Altman DG. Better reporting of randomised control trials : the CONSORT statement. *British Medical Journal* 1996; 313 (7057), 570-571.

Appleton DR. Detecting poor design, erroneous analysis and misinterpretation of studies. *Journal of Evaluation in Clinical Practice* 1995; 1(2) : 113-118

Avis M. Reading research critically. II. An introduction to appraisal : assessing the evidence. *Journal of Clinical Nursing* 1994; 3 : 271-277.

Baumgartner TA and Strong CH. *Conducting and reading research in health and human performance.* Madison, Wisconsin : Brown & Benchmark, 1994.

Begg C et al. Improving the quality of reporting of randomized control trials : the CONSORT statement. *JAMA* 1996 Aug 28; 276 (8):

Bero LA and Rennie D. Influences on the quality of published drug studies. *International Journal of Technology Assessment In Health Care* 1996; 12 (2) : 209-237.

Cook DJ, Guyatt GH, Laupacis A et al. Rules of evidence and clinical recommendations on the use of antithrombotic agents. *Chest* 1992; 102 : 305S- 311S.

Cook DJ, Sackett DL and Spitzer WO. Methodologic guidelines for systematic reviews of randomised control trials in health care from the Potsdam Consultation on Meta-analysis. *Journal of Clinical Epidemiology* 1995; 48 (1) : 167-71.

DuRant RH. Checklist for the evaluation of research articles. *Journal of Adolescent Health* 1994; 15 : 4-8.

Hutton JL. The ethics of randomised controlled trials : a matter of statistical belief? *Health Care Analysis* 1996 May; 4(2) 95-102

Jadad AR et al. Assessing the quality of reports of randomized clinical trials - is blinding necessary? *Controlled Clinical Trials* 1996; 17 (1) : 1-12.

Jadad AR and McQuay HJ. Meta-analyses to evaluate analgesic interventions : a systematic qualitative review of their methodology. *Journal of Clinical Epidemiology* 1996 Feb; 49(2) : 235-243

Jones B, Jarvis P, Lewes JA et al. Trials to assess equivalence : the importance of rigorous methods. *BMJ* 1996 Jul 6; 313 (7048) : 36-39.

Khan KS, Daya A and Jadad AL. The importance of quality of primary studies in producing unbiased systematic reviews. *Archives of Internal Medicine* 1996 Mar 25; 156 (6) : 661-666.

Lau J and Chalmers TC . The rational use of therapeutic drugs in the 21st century. Important lessons from cumulative meta-analyses of randomized control trials. *International Journal of Technology Assessment in Health Care* 1995 Summer; 11(3) : 509-22

Milne R and Chambers L. Assessing the scientific quality of review articles. *Journal of Epidemiology and Community Health* 1993; 47 : 169-170

Moher D. Facilitating clinical research in the 1990s and beyond : challenges facing clinical trial registers. *Fundamentals of Clinical Pharmacology* 1995; 9(4) : 381-3

Moher D, Fortin P, Jadad AR et al. Completeness of reporting of trials published in languages other than English : implications for conduct and reporting of systematic reviews. *Lancet*. 1996 Feb 10; 347(8998) : 363-366.

Moher D and Olkin I. Meta-analysis of randomized controlled trials. A concern for standards; [comment]. Comment on : *JAMA* 1995 Dec 27;274(24):1935-8. Comment on : JAMA 1995 Dec 27;274(24):1942-8. *Journal of the American Medical Association* 1995 Dec 27; 274(24) : 1962-4

Moher D, Jadad AR, Nichol G et al. Assessing the quality of randomised controlled trials : an annotated bibliography of scales and checklists. *Controlled Clinical Trials* 1995; 16 : 62-73.

Moher D, Jadad AR and Tugwell P. Assessing the quality of Randomized Controlled Trials - current issues and future directions. *International Journal of Technology Assessment in Health Care* 1996; 12 (2) : 195-208.

Nony P, Cucherat M, Haugh MC et al. Critical reading of the meta-analysis of clinical trials. *Therapie*. 1995 Jul-Aug; 50 (4) : 339-51

Oxman AD. Checklists for review articles. *British Medical Journal* 1994; 309 : 648-51.

Oxman AD and Guyatt GH. Guidelines for reading literature reviews. *Canadian Medical Association Journal* 1988; 138 : 697-703.

Oxman AD and Guyatt GH. Validation of an index of the quality of review articles. *Journal of Clinical Epidemiology* 1991; 44 : 1271-8.

Oxman AD, Guyatt GH, Singer J et al. Agreement among reviewers of review articles. *Journal of Clinical Epidemiology* 1991; 44 : 91-8.

Oxman AD, Guyatt GH, Cook DJ et al. An index of scientific quality for health reports in the lay press. *Journal of Clinical Epidemiology* 1993; 46 (9) 987-1001

Sackett DL, Haynes RB, Guyatt GH et al. *Clinical epidemiology : a basic science for clinical medicine*. 2nd edition. Boston : Little, Brown and Co, 1991.

Sacristan JA, Soto J and Galende I. Evaluation of pharmacoeconomic studies : utilisation of a checklist. *Annals of Phamacotherapy* 1993; 27 : 1126-33.

Schulz KF. Randomised trials, human nature, and reporting guidelines. *Lancet* 1996 Aug 31; 348 (9027) : 596-598

Schulz KF, Chalmers I, Hayes RJ, et al : Empirical evidence of bias : Dimensions of methodological quality associated with estimates of treatment effects in controlled trials. *Journal of the American Medical Association* 1995;273:408-412.

Schulz KF et al. Assessing the quality of randomisation from reports of controlled trials published in obstetrics and gynaecology reports. *Journal of the American Medical Association* 1994; 272 : 125-128.

Streiner DL. A checklist for evaluating the usefulness of rating scales. *Canadian Journal of Psychiatry* 1993; 38:140-8.

PUBLICATION BIAS

Dickersin K. The existence of publication bias and risk factors for its occurrence. *JAMA* 1990; 263 : 1385-1389.

Dickersin K, Min YI and Meinert CL.. Factors influencing publication of research results : follow up of applications submitted to two institutional boards. *JAMA* 1992; 267 : 374-378.

Dickersin K and Min YI. NIH clinical trials and publication bias. *Online Journal of Current Clinical Trials* (serial online). Apr 28, 1993 : 50.

Easterbrook PJ, Berlin JA, Gopalan R et al. Publication bias in clinical research. *Lancet* 1991; 337 : 867-872.

Gilbody S and House A. Publication bias and meta-analysis [letter]. *British Journal of Psychiatry*. 1995 Aug; 167(2) : 266

Gregoire G, Derderian F and LeLorier J. Selecting the language of the publications included in a meta-analysis : is there a Tower of Babel bias? *Journal of Clinical Epidemiology* 1995; 48 (1) : 159-166.

Hutchison BG, Oxman AD and Lloyd S. Comprehensiveness and bias in reporting clinical trials. Study of reviews of pneumococcal vaccine effectiveness. *Canadian Family Physician*. 1995 Aug; 41 : 1356-60.

Moher D et al. Completeness of reporting of trials published in languages other than English : implications for conduct and reporting of systematic reviews. *Lancet* 1996 Feb 10; 347 (8998) : 363-366.

Scherer RW, Dickersin K and Langenberg P : Full publication of results initially presented in abstracts : a meta-analysis. *Journal of the American Medical Association* 1994; 272:158-162.

Stewart LA and Parmar MKB. Bias in the analysis and reporting of randomized controlled trials. *International Journal of Technology Assessment in Health Care* 1996; 2 (2) : 264-275.

PRESENTATION OF RESULTS

Bobbio M et al. Completeness of reporting trial results : effect on physicians' willingness to prescribe. *Lancet* 1994 : 343 : 1209-1212.

Braitman LE and Davidoff F. Predicting clinical states in individual patients. *Annals of Internal Medicine* 1996; 125 (5) : 406-412.

Bucher HC, Weinbacher M and Gyr K. Influence of method of reporting study results on decision of physicians to prescribe drugs to lower cholesterol concentration. *British Medical Journal* 1995; 309 : 761-764.

Cook RJ and Sackett DL. The number needed to treat : a clinically useful measure of treatment effect. *British Medical Journal* 1995; 310 : 452-454.

Entwistle V. Reporting research in medical journals and newspapers. *British Medical Journal* 1995; 310 : 920-22.

Fahey T, Griffiths S and Peters TJ. Evidence based purchasing : Understanding results of clinical trials and systematic reviews. *British Medical Journal* 1995; 311:1056-1060.

Guyatt G, Jaeschke R, Heddle N et al. Basic statistics for clinicians : 1. Hypothesis testing. *Canadian Medical Association Journal* 1995 Jan 1; 152 (1) : 27-32.

Guyatt G, Jaeschke R, Heddle N et al. Basic statistics for clinicians : 2. Interpreting study results : confidence intervals. *Canadian Medical Association Journal* 1995 Jan 15; 152(2) : 169-173.

Guyatt G, Walter S, Shannon H et al. Basic statistics for clinicians : 4. Correlation and regression. *Canadian Medical Association Journal* 1995 Feb 15; 152(4) : 497-504.

Jaeschke R, Guyatt G, Shannon H et al. Basic statistics for clinicians : 3. Assessing the effects of treatments : measures of association. *Canadian Medical Association Journal* 1995 Feb 1; 152(3) : 351-357.

Laupacis A, Sackett DL and Roberts RS. An assessment of clinically useful measures of the consequences of treatment. *New England Journal of Medicine* 1988; 318 : 1728-1733.

Laupacis A, Naylor CD and Sackett DL. How should the results of clinical trials be presented to clinicians? [editorial] *ACP Journal Club* 1992 May/June; A12-A14

Naylor CD. Measured enthusiasm : does the method of reporting trial results alter perceptions of therapeutic effectiveness? *Annals of Internal Medicine* 1992; 117 : 916-921.

Sackett DL. On some clinically useful measures of the effects of treatment. *Evidence Based Medicine* 1996; 1 (2):37-38.

Sackett D and Cook RJ. Understanding clinical trials : what measures of efficacy should journal articles provide busy clinicians? *British Medical Journal* 1994 Sep 24; 309 : 755-756.

Sackett DL, Deeks JJ and Altman DG. Down with odds ratios! (EBM Notebook). *Evidence Based Medicine* 1996; 1 (6) : 164-166

SBU - Newsletter English edition. Turning molehills into mountains. On World Wide Web at : *http://www.sbu.se/newsletter/articles/moleshills.html*

SBU - Newsletter English edition. Science or propaganda? On World Wide Web at : *http://www.sbu.se/newsletter/articles/scienceor.html*

Sinclair JC and Bracken MB. Clinically useful measures of effect in binary analyses of randomized trials. *Journal of Clinical Epidemiology* 1994; 47 : 881-90.

Sullivan FM. and MacNaughton RJ. Evidence in consultations : interpreted and individualised. 1996 Oct 5; *Lancet* 348 (9032) : 941-943.

Wiffen PJ and Moore RA. Demonstrating effectiveness - the concept of numbers-needed-to-treat. *Journal of Clinical Pharmacy and Therapeutics* 1996 Feb; 21 (1) : 23-27.

DISSEMINATION AND CHANGING PRACTICE

Abbott P and Sapsford R. (eds). *Research into Practice : a reader for nurses and the caring professions.* Oxford : Oxford University Press, 1992.

Agency for Health Care Policy and Research. *Information dissemination to health care practitioners and policymakers.* Bethesda, Maryland : Agency for Health Care Policy and Research, 1992.

Anglia and Oxford Regional Health Authority. *Getting research into practice and purchasing (GRIPP), Four Counties Approach. Resource Pack.* Oxford : Anglia and Oxford RHA, 1994.

Bernstein RM, Hollingworth GR and Wood WE. Prompting physicians for cost effective test ordering in the low prevalence conditions of family medicine. *Journal of the American Medical Informatics Association,* 1994; SS : 824-828.

Black N and Thompson E. Obstacles to medical audit : British doctors speak. *Social Science and Medicine* 1993; 36 (7) : 849-856.

Budd J and Dawson S. *Influencing clinical practice : implementation of R&D results.* London : Management School, Imperial College, 1994.

Closs SJ and Cheater F. Utilisation of nursing research. *Journal of Advanced Nursing* 1994; 19 : 762-773.

Crosswaite C and Curtice L. Disseminating research results - the challenge of bridging the gap between research and health action. *Health Promotion International* 1994; 9 : 289-296.

Davis DA, Thompson MA, Oxman AD, Haynes RB. Evidence for the effectiveness of CME : a review of 50 randomized controlled trials. *JAMA* 1992; 268 : 1111-1117.

Davis DA, Thomson MA, Oxman AD, et al. Changing physician performance : A systematic review of the effect of continuing medical education strategies. *Journal of the American Medical Association* 1995;274:700-705.

Davis P and Howden-Chapman P. Translating research findings into health policy. *Social Science and Medicine* 1996 Sep; 43 (5) : 865-872.

Department of Health. *Taking research seriously : means of improving and assessing the use and dissemination of research.* London : HMSO, 1990.

Department of Health. *Methods to promote the implementation of research findings in the NHS - Priorities for Evaluation.* London : HMSO, 1995.

Dickson R. Dissemination and implementation : the wider picture. *Nurse Researcher* 1996; 4 (1) : 4-14

Dopson S, Mant J and Hicks N. Getting research into practice : facing the issues. *Journal of Management in Medicine* 1994; 8 (6) : 4-12.

Dowie J. The research practice gap and the role of decision analysis in closing it. *Health Care Analysis* 1996; 4 : 1-14.

Dunning M, McQuay H and Milne R. Getting a GRiP. *Health Service Journal* 1994 Apr 24; 104 (5400) : 24-25.

Dunn EV, Norton PG, Stewart M, Tudiver F, Bass MJ. *Disseminating research/changing practice.* (Research Methods in Primary Care Volume 6). London : Sage, 1994.

Effective Health Care. Implementing Clinical Practice Guidelines : can guidelines be used to improve clinical practice? *Effective Health Care Bulletin* Number 8. University of Leeds, Leeds, 1995.

Eve R, Golton I, Hodgkin P et al. Beyond guidelines : promoting clinical change in the real world. *Journal of Management in Medicine* 1996; 10 (1) : 16-25.

Freemantle N and Watt I. Dissemination : implementing the findings of research. *Health Libraries Review.* 1994; 11(2) : 133-137

Gagliardi A. Ontario Health Care Evaluation Network [OHCEN] : building partnerships, promoting evidence. *Bibliotheca medica canadiana* 1996 Fall; 18 (1) : 14-17.

Goldberg HI, Cummings MA, Steinberg EP et al. Deliberations on the dissemination of PORT products : translating research findings into improved patient outcomes. *Medical Care* 1994; 32 (Suppl. 7) : JS90-JS110.

Goodman GR. Group processes of decision making for hospital-based technology assessment committees. *Biomed-Instrum-Technol.* 1995 Sep-Oct; 29(5) : 410-7

Greco PJ and Eisenberg JM. Changing physicians' practices. *New England Journal of Medicine* 1993; 329 : 1271-1274.

Grimshaw JM and Russell IT. Achieving health gain through clinical guidelines. II. Ensuring guidelines change medical practice. *Quality in Health Care* 1994; 3 : 45-52.

Guyatt GH, Cook DJ and Jaeschke RZ. How should clinicians use the results of randomized trials? *ACP Journal Club* 1995 Jan-Feb; 122 (1) : A10-A11.

Guyatt GH, Jaeschke RZ and Cook DJ. Applying the findings of clinical trials to individual patients. *ACP Journal Club* 1995 Mar-Apr; 122 (2) : A12-A13.

Gyte G. Putting research into practice in maternity care. *Modern Midwife* 1994; 4 : 19-20

Haines A. The science of perpetual change. *British Journal of General Practice* 1996; 46 (403) : 115-119.

Haines A and Jones R. Implementing findings of research. *British Medical Journal* 1994; 308 : 1489-1492.

Harrison S. Knowledge into practice : what's the problem? *Journal of Management in Medicine* 1994; 8 (2) : 9-16.

Haynes RB, Hayward RSA and Lomas J. Bridges between healthcare research evidence and clinical practice. *Journal of The American Medical Informatics Association* 1995; 2 (6) : 342-350. Also available as *Bridges between Evidence and Practice.* on the Internet at :
http://hiru.mcmaster.ca/ebm/informat/bridges.htm

Haynes, RB, Sackett, DL, Gray, JMA.et al. Transferring evidence from research into practice : 1. The role of clinical care research evidence in clinical decisions. *Evidence-Based Medicine* 1996 Nov-Dec; 1 (7) : 196-198.

Hirsh J and Haynes B. Transforming evidence into practice : evidence-based consensus. *ACP Journal Club* 1993 Jan-Feb; 118 : A-16.

Hodgkins P, Eve R, Golton I et al. Changing clinical behaviour on a city-wide scale : lessons from the FACTS project. *Journal of Clinical Effectiveness* 1996; 1 (1) : 8-10.

Hyde CJ. Using the evidence : a need for quantity, not quality? *International Journal of Technology Assessment in Health Care* 1996; 12 (2) : 280-287.

Ibbotson SL, Long AF, Sheldon TA et al. An initial evaluation of effective health care bulletins as instruments of effective dissemination. *Journal of Management in Medicine* 1993; 7 : 48-57.

Joint initiative to share practice developments. *Nursing Standard* 1996 Jul 24th; 10 (44) : 32.

Kasper J, Mulley A and Wennberg J. Developing shared decision programmes to improve the quality of health care. *Quality Review Bulletin* 1992; 18 : 182-190.

Kitson A. From research to practice : one organizational model for promoting reseaerch-based practice. *Journal of Advanced Nursing* 1996 Mar; 23 (3) : 430-440.

Lomas J. Diffusion, dissemination and implementation : who should do what? *Annals of the New York Academy of Sciences* 1994; 226-237.

Lomas J and Haynes RB. A taxonomy and critical review of tested strategies for the application of clinical practice recommendations : from "official" to "individual" clinical policy. *American Journal of Preventive Medicine* 1988; 4 (4 suppl) 77-94, discussion 95-7.

Long AF. Health services research - a radical approach to crossing the research and development divide? In Baker MR and Kirk S. *Making Sense of Research and Development.* Oxford : Radcliffe Medical Press, 1996.

MacGuire JM. Putting nursing research findings into practice : research utilization as an aspect of the management of change. *Journal of Advanced Nursing* 1990; 15 : 614-620.

Mittman BS, Tonesk X and Jacobson PD. Implementing clinical practice guidelines : social influence strategies and practitioner behaviour change. *Quality Review Bulletin* 1992; 18 : 413-422.

Mugford M et al. Effects of feedback of information on clinical practice : a review. *British Medical Journal* 1991; 303 : 398-402.

Needham G. A GRiPPing yarn - getting research into practice : a case study. *Health Libraries Review* 1994; 11 : 269-277.

Oxman AD, Thomson MA, Davis DA et al. No magic bullets : a systematic review of 102 trials of interventions to help health care professionals deliver services more effectively or efficiently. *Canadian Medical Association Journal* 1995; 153 (10) : 1423-1431.

Oxman AD. *A systematic review of interventions to improve the performance of health care professions.* London : NHS Executive (North Thames) Research and Development Directorate, 1995.

Paes BA, Modi A and Dunmore R. Changing physicians' behaviour using combined strategies and an evidence-based protocol. *Archives of Paediatric and Adolescent Medicine* 1994; 148 (12) : 1277-1280.

Paterson-Brown S, Wyatt J and Fisk N. Are clinicians interested in up-to-date reviews of effective care? *British Medical Journal* 1993; 307 (6917) : 1464.

Paterson-Brown S, Fisk NM and Wyatt JC. Uptake of meta-analytical overviews of effective care in English obstetric units. *British Journal of Obstetrics and Gynaecology* 1995; 102 : 297-301.

Peters DA. Implementation of research findings. *Health Bulletin* 1992 : 50 : 68-77.

Promoting the implementation of research findings in the NHS. *NAHAT Briefing* 1995 November; 89.

Robertson N, Baker R and Hearnshaw H. Changing the clinical behaviour of doctors : a psychological framework. *Quality in Health Care* 1996 Mar; 5 (1) : 51-54.

Rogers EM. *Diffusion of innovations.* 4th ed. New York : Free Press, 1995.

Sackett DL. Applying overviews and meta-analyses at the bedside. *Journal of Clinical Epidemiology* 1995; 48 (1) : 61-66. [Discussion by Chalmers I, p.67].

Stocking B. Why research findings are not used by commissions - and what can be done about it. *Journal of Public Health Medicine* 1995; 17 (4) : 380-382.

Stocking B. Promoting change in clinical care. *Quality in Health Care* 1992; 1(1) : 56-60.

Stocking B. Implementing the findings of *Effective Care in Pregnancy and Childbirth. Milbank Quarterly* 1993; 71 : 497-522.

Sullivan FM and MacNaughton RJ. Evidence in consultations : interpreted and individualised. *Lancet* 1996; 348 (9032) : 941-943.

Tanenbaum SJ. Knowing and acting in medical practice : the epistemiological politics of outcomes research. *Journal of Health Politics, Policy and Law* 1994; 19 (1) : 27-44.

Van Amringe M and Shannon TE. Awareness, assimilation and adoption : the challenge of effective dissemination : the first AHCPR-sponsored guidelines. *Quality Review Bulletin* 1992; 18 : 302-316.

Vaughn B and Edwards M. *Interface between Research and Practice*. London : King's Fund, 1995.

Watt I. The dissemination of R&D information. *IFMH Inform* 1996; 7 (1) : 1-4

Williamson P. From dissemination to use : management and organisational barriers to the application of health services research findings. *Health Bulletin* 1992; 50 : 78-86.

GUIDELINES

Antrobus S and Brown S. Guidelines and Protocols : a chance to take the lead. *Nursing Times* 1996 Jun 5; 92 (23) : 38-39.

Ayres P, Renvoize T and Robinson M. Clinical guidelines : key decisions for acute service providers. *British Journal of Health Care Management* 1995; 1 (11) : 547-551.

Browman GP et al. The Practice Guidelines development cycle - a conceptual tool for Practice Guidelines development and implementation. *Journal of Clinical Oncology*, 1995, 13 (2) : 502-512

Cluzeau F, Littlejohns P and Grimshaw JM. Appraising clinical guidelines : towards a "Which" guide for purchasers. *Quality in Health Care* 1994; 3 : 121-122

Deighan M and Hitch S. *Clinical Effectiveness : from guidelines to cost-effective practice.* Brentwood, Essex : Earlybrave Publications Limited, 1995. [ISBN : 1-900432-00-5]

Delamothe T. Wanted : guidelines that doctors will follow : implementation is the problem. *British Medical Journal* 1993; 307 : 218

Duff LA et al. Clinical guidelines : an introduction to their development and implementation. *Journal of Advanced Nursing* 1996 May; 23 (5) : 887-895

Eccles M et al. Developing valid guidelines : methodological and procedural issues from the North of England Evidence Based Guidelines Development Project. *Quality in Health Care* 1996; 5 (1) : 44-50.

Eccles M. North of England Evidence Based Guidelines Development Project : summary of evidence based guideline for the primary care management of asthma in adults. *British Medical Journal* 1996; 312 (7033) : 762-766.

Eccles M , Clapp Z, Grimshaw J et al. North of England Evidence Based Guidelines Development Project : methods of guideline development. *British Medical Journal* 1996 Mar 23; 312 (7033) : 760-762.

Eddy DM. Guidelines for policy statements : the explicit approach. *JAMA* 1990; 263 : 2239-2243.

Eddy DM. Designing a practice policy : standards, guidelines and options. *JAMA* 1990; 263 : 3077-3084.

Effective Health Care. Implementing clinical practice guidelines : can guidelines be used to improve clinical practice.? *Effective Health Care Bulletin* Number 8. University of Leeds, Leeds, 1995.

Feder G. Clinical guidelines in 1994 : let's be careful out there. *British Medical Journal* 1994; 309 : 1457-1458.

Ferguson JH. The NIH Consensus Development Program : the evolution of guidelines. *International Journal of Technology Assessment in Health Care* 1996; 12 (3) : 460

Field MJ and Lohr KN. *Clinical practice guidelines : from development to use.* Washington DC: National Academy Press, 1990.

Grimshaw J, Eccles M and Russell I . Developing clinically valid practice guidelines. *Journal of Evaluation in Clinical Practice* 1995; 1 (1) : 37-48.

Grimshaw J, Freemantle N , Wallace S et al. Developing and implementing clinical practice guidelines. *Quality in Health Care* 1995; 4 : 55-64.

Grimshaw JM and Hutchinson A. Clinical practice guidelines - do they enhance value for money in health care. *British Medical Bulletin*, 1995 Oct; 51 (4) : 927-940.

Grimshaw JM and Russell IT. Achieving health gain through clinical guidelines. I. Developing scientifically valid guidelines. *Quality in Health Care* 1994; 2 : 243-248.

Grimshaw JM and Russell IT. Achieving health gain through clinical guidelines. II. Ensuring guidelines change medical practice. *Quality in Health Care* 1994; 3 : 45-52

Grimshaw JM and Russell IT. Effect of clinical guidelines on medical practice : a systematic review of rigorous evaluations. *Lancet* 1993; 342 : 1317-1322.

Hayward J. Purchasing clinically effective care. *British Medical Journal* 1994; 309 : 823-4.

Hayward RSA and Laupacis A. Initiating, conducting and maintaining guidelines development programs. *Canadian Medical Association Journal* 1993; 148 : 507-512.

Hopkins A. Some reservations about clinical guidelines. *Archives of Disease in Childhood* 1995; 72 (1) : 70-75.

Humphris D and Littlejohns P. Implementing clinical guidelines : linking and learning from clinical audit. *Audit Trends* 1996 Jun; 4 (2) : 59-62

Klazinga N. Compliance with practice guidelines : clinical autonomy revisited. *Health Policy* 1994; 28 : 51-66.

Little P et al. General practitioners' management of acute back pain : a survey of reported practice compared with clinical guidelines. *British Medical Journal* 1996; 312 (7029) : 485-488.

Mansfield CD. Attitudes and behaviours toward clinical guidelines : the clinicians perspective. *Quality in Health Care* 1996; 4 : 250-255.

Marriott S. Clinical practice guidelines : who needs them? *Psychiatric Bulletin* 1995 Jul; 19 (7) : 403-406.

Marriott S and Lelliott P. *Clinical practice guidelines and their development.* Council Report CR 34. London : Royal College of Psychiatrists, 1994.

Marriott S and Palmer C. Clinical practice guidelines : on what evidence is our clinical practice based? *Psychiatric Bulletin* 1996 Jun; 20 (6) : 363-366.

McKee M and Clarke A. Guidelines, enthusiasms, uncertainty, and the limits to purchasing. *British Medical Journal* 1995; 310 : 101-104.

Muirhead N et al. Evidence-based recommendations for the clinical use of recombinant human erythropoietin. *American Journal of Kidney Diseases* 1995; 26 (2) : S1-S24

Onion CWR et al. Local clinical guidelines. *Family Practice* 1996 Feb; 13 (1) : 28-34.

Palmer C. Clinical practice guidelines : the priorities. *Psychiatric Bulletin* 1996 Jan; 20 (1) : 40-42.

Sheldon TA and Borowitz M. Changing the measure of quality in the NHS : from purchasing activity to purchasing protocols. *Quality in Health Care* 1993; 2 : 149-150.

Swales JD. Guidelines on guidelines. *Journal of Hypertension* 1993; 11 : 899-903.

Thompson C. The College's (Royal College of Psychiatrists) Clinical Guideline Development Programme. *Psychiatric Bulletin* 1995 Jul; 19 (7) : 401-402.

Thomson R, Lavender M and Madhok R. How to ensure that guidelines are effective. *British Medical Journal* 1995 Jul 22; 311 (6999) : 237-242.

HEALTH TECHNOLOGY ASSESSMENT - OVERVIEWS

Assessing the effects of health technologies. London : Research and Development Division, Department of Health, 1992.

Smith R. Towards a knowledge based health service : priorities for health technology assessment. *British Medical Journal* 1994; 309 : 217

Stevens A, Robert G and Gabbay J. Identifying new health care technologies in the United Kingdom. *International Journal of Technology Assessment in Health Care* 1997 13 (1) : 59-67.

US Congress, Office of Technology Assessment. *Identifying health technologies that work : searching for the evidence*, OTA-H-608. Washington, DC : US Government Printing Office, September 1994.

THE CONSUMER DIMENSION

Buckland S and Gann B. *Disseminating treatment outcomes information to consumers.* (Promoting Patient Choice No. 4). London : King's Fund, 1996.

Coulter A. Assembling the evidence : patient-focused outcomes research. *Health Libraries Review* 1994; 11 : 263-268.

Dunning M and Needham G (eds). *But will it work, doctor?* Milton Keynes, Consumer Health Information Consortium, 1993.

Entwistle V, Gann R, Lefebvre C et al. Sharing outcomes information with consumers : a new course for health librarians. *Health Libraries Review* 1994; 11 (4) : 279-282.

Entwistle VA, Sheldon TA, Sowden AS et al. Supporting consumer involvement in decisionmaking : what constitutes quality in consumer information? *International Journal of Quality in Health Care* [In press].

Entwistle V, Watt IS and Herring JE. *Information about health care effectiveness : an introduction for consumer health information providers.* (Promoting Patient Choice No. 3). London : King's Fund, 1996.

Gann B. Information for patients and carers on the effectiveness of treatments. *Outcomes Briefing* 1996 Oct; (8) : 38-41.

Gann B. Consumers and evidence-based health care. *Evidence-Based Purchasing* 1995 Aug; (9) : 1.

Hope T. *Evidence-based patient choice. Report to the Anglia and Oxford RHA into the uses of evidence based information for enhancing patient choice.* Oxford : October 1995.

Hope T. *Evidence-based patient choice.*(Promoting Patient Choice). London : King's Fund, 1996.

Hyatt J. *In it together : promoting information for shared decision making.* London : King's Fund, 1994.

Informed choice. *Purchasing in Practice* 1996 Feb; (7); 18-19

Meerabeau L. The role of 'consumers'/users in evidence based health care. *Journal of Interprofessional Care* 1996; 10 (2) : 198.

Muir Gray JA. Evidence-based patient choice and clinical practice. In:- *Evidence-based health care : how to make health policy and management decisions*, by JA Muir Gray. London : Churchill Livingstone, 1997. 201-220.

Needham G. But will it work doctor?, 1996. *Outcomes Briefing* 1996 Oct; (8):35-38.

Oliver S, Rajan L, Turner H et al. Informed choice for users of health services : views on ultrasonography leaflets of women in early pregnancy, midwives, and ultrasonographers. *British Medical Journal* 1996 Nov 16; 313 (7067) : 1251-1253.

Promoting Action on Clinical Effectiveness (PACE). Involving patients. *PACE Bulletin.* 1996 Sep; (Special Issue) : 1-4.

Rigge M. Clinical audit and the availability of evidence-based care : the patient's view. In : Miles A and Lugon M (eds) *Effective Clinical Practice.* Oxford : Blackwell Science, 1996 : 237-247.

Rosser J, Watt IS and Entwistle V. Informed choice initiative : an example of reaching users with evidence-based information. *Journal of Clinical Effectiveness* 1996; 1 (4) : 143-145.

Social Science Research Unit. *A pilot study of 'Informed Choice' leaflets on positions in labour and routine ultrasound.* CRD Report 6. York : University of York, 1997.

Thompson H. *Dissemination of Mental Health Outcomes.* (Promoting Patient Choice No. 8) London : King's Fund, 1997.

Torgerson DJ, Klaber-Moffett J and Russell IT. Patient preferences in randomised trials : threat or opportunity? *Journal of Health Services Research & Policy* 1996 Oct; 1 (4), 194-197

ECONOMIC EVALUATION - INTRODUCTORY

Adams ME, McCall NT, Gray DT et al. Economic analysis in randomized control trials. *Medical Care* 1992; 30 (3) 231-243.

Backhouse ME, Backhouse RJ and Edey SA. Economic evaluation bibliography. *Health Economics* 1992 Dec; 1 (Suppl) : 1-235.

BMJ publishes guidelines for economic evaluations. *OHE News* Autumn 1996; (4) : 1,7.

Briggs A, Sculpher M and Buxton MJ. Uncertainty in the economic evaluation of health care technologies : the role of sensitivity analysis. *Health Economics* 1994; 3 : 95-104.

Clancy CM and Kamerow-DB. Evidence-based medicine meets cost-effectiveness analysis [editorial]. *JAMA*. 1996 Jul 24-31; 276(4) : 329-30

Coyle D. *Increasing the impact of economic evaluations on health-care decision-making.* York. Centre for Health Economics, 1993.

Coyle D and Davies L. How to assess cost-effectiveness : elements of a sound economic evaluation. In : Drummond MF and Maynard A. *Purchasing and providing cost-effective health care.* Edinburgh : Churchill Livingstone, 1993 : 66-79.

Department of Health, Economics and Operational Research Division. *Register of cost-effectiveness studies.* Leeds : DoH,1994.

Drummond MF. Common mistakes in the design of economic evaluations of medicines. *British Journal of Medical Economics* 1991; 1 : 5-14

Drummond MF. *Economic analysis alongside controlled trials : an introduction for clinical researchers.* Leeds : Department of Health, 1994.

Drummond MF, Brandt A, Luce BR et al. Standardizing economic evaluation methodologies in health care. *International Journal of Technology Assessment in Health Care* 1993; 9 : 26-36.

Drummond MF and Davies LM. Economic analysis alongside clinical trials : revisiting the methodological issues. *International Journal of Technology Assessment in Health Care* 1991; 7 (4) : 561-573.

Drummond MF, Stoddart GL and Torrance GW. *Methods for the economic evaluation of health care programmes.* Oxford, Oxford Medical Publications, 1987.

Gafni A. Economic evaluation of health care interventions : an economist's perspective [editorial]. *ACP Journal Club* 1996 Mar-Apr : A12-A14.

Gold MR. *Cost-effectiveness in health and medicine.* Oxford : Oxford University Press, 1996.

International Working Party. [Guidelines for authors and peer reviewers for health economics studies]. BMJ 1996 Aug 3; 313 (7052).

Kobelt G. *Health economics : an introduction to economic evaluation.* London, Office of Health Economics, 1996.

Lockett T. *Health economics for the uninitiated.* Oxford : Radcliffe Medical Press, 1996.

Luce BR and Simpson K. Methods of cost-effectiveness analysis : areas of consensus and debate. *Clinical Therapeutics* 1995; 17 : 109-125.

McGhan WF and Lewis JW. Guidelines for pharmacoeconomic studies. *Clinical Therapeutics* 1993; 14 : 486-494

Naylor D. Cost-effectiveness analysis : are the outputs worth the inputs? *ACP Journal Club* 1996; 124 (1) : A12-A14.

Robinson R. Economic evaluation and health care : what does it mean? *British Medical Journal* 1993; 307 (6905) : 670-673

Robinson R. Costs and cost-minimisation analysis. *British Medical Journal* 1993; 307 (6906) : 726-8.

Robinson R. Cost-effectiveness analysis. *British Medical Journal* 1993; 307 (6907) : 793-5.

Robinson R. Cost-utility analysis. *British Medical Journal* 1993; 307 (6908) : 859-862

Robinson R. Cost-benefit analysis. *British Medical Journal* 1993; 307 (6909) : 924-6.

Robinson R. The policy context. *British Medical Journal* 1993; 307 (6910) : 994-6.

Sacristan JA, Soto J and Galende I. Evaluation of pharmacoeconomic studies : utilization of a checklist. *Annals of Pharmacotherapy* 1993; 27 : 1126-1133.

Stoddart GL and Drummond MF. How to read clinical journals : VII. To understand an economic evaluation (part D). *Canadian Medical Association Journal* 1984; 130 : 1542-1540.

Udvarhelyi IS, Colditz GA, Rai A et al. Cost-effectiveness and cost-benefit analysis in the medical literature : are methods being used correctly? *Annals of Internal Medicine* 1992; 116 : 238-242.

Evidence-based Practice Resource Guide

The diversity of media available to support Evidence Based Practice has necessitated a change in format for this Resource Guide. Instead of splitting resources according to format the guide now lists them in alphabetical order and then provides a key to the types of resource available for each entry. The types listed are as follows:-

Type	Definition
Book	A substantive publication issued on an ad hoc basis
Bulletin	Thematic newsletter covering individual topics
CD-ROM Database	Product supplied on Compact Disk
Computer Assisted Learning	Stand-alone or Internet resource for non-mediated learning
Discussion List	Internet-based discussion forum
Information Service	A formally-organised information provider
Journal	A substantial periodic publication
Newsletter	A brief periodic publication
Online Database	Database available via modem and/or Internet
Online Journal	Journal available via modem and/or Internet
Organisation	A contact point that will answer basic enquiries
Project	A time-limited initiative exploring specific issues.
Software	Products supplied on floppy disk or downloadable via ftp
Training Course Provider	An organisation providing training courses
Training materials	Handouts or other teaching materials for mediated learning
WWW database	A searchable World Wide Web interface
WWW presence	World Wide Web Pages with basic information only
WWW resource list	A set of links to other World Wide Web sites
WWW site	World Wide Web Pages including publications etcetera

Abstracts of Clinical Care Guidelines

A publication of the Joint Commission (JCAHO) that abstracts guidelines with details of sources. Published 10 times a year it costs $95 per year. The newsletter is not indexed elsewhere but does publish a self-index in its November-December issue. Available from Mosby on 1-800-453-4351. *Type of Resource:- Newsletter*

ACP Journal Club (ISSN: 0003-4819)

ACP Journal Club is a bimonthly journal whose general purpose is to select from the biomedical literature those articles reporting studies and reviews that warrant immediate attention by physicians attempting to keep pace with important advances in internal medicine. These articles are summarized in "value added" abstracts and commented on by clinical experts. The database [see below under *Best Evidence*] 1991-1995 contains almost 900 articles to support the practice of evidence based healthcare. Articles are of two types; editorials on aspects of using the evidence and comprehensive summaries of significant articles from 50 of medicine's most influential journals. Each summary is followed by an expert commentary that places the summary in practice perspective. *Type of resource* : *WWW site; Journal; Software.*

http://www.acponline.org/journals/acpjc/jcmenu.htm

A UK mirror site exists at the Centre for Evidence Based Medicine:-

http:// http://cebm.jr2.ox.ac.uk/docs/hiru/acpjc/default.htm

ACP Library on Disk

Compact disk from the American College of Physicians containing *Best Evidence* [see below], ACP approved Clinical Practice Guidelines, Common Diagnostic Tests, Common Screening Tests plus other texts representing over 7,000 pages of clinical information. The database is available for $229 (non-members) from the Customer Service Center, American College of Physicians, Independence Mall West, Sixth Street at Race, Philadelphia, PA 19106. Tel : (800 523-1546 ext 2600). *Type of resource* : *CD-ROM Database.*

Agency for Health Care Policy and Research

This site includes practice guidelines in three forms; full version, clinician's guide and patients guide. *Type of resource* : *WWW site, Online Database.*

http://www.ahcpr.gov/

Arcus Statistical Package

This downloadable statistics package can be placed on a local machine and then used to calculate odds ratios, relative risk and other clinical measures such as Numbers Needed to Treat. It includes exact confidence intervals for all of these which is very rare. The package also includes calculation of pooled odds ratios using the Mantel-Haenszel or Woolf method. It is made available by Dr Iain Buchan, formerly of the Departments of Medicine and Primary Care, University of Liverpool. Arcus Biomedical for Windows is about to be launched. Details of the beta site can be obtained from Iain Buchan, now at Institute of Public Health, University of Cambridge.(E-mail:- ieb21@cam.ac.uk). *Type of resource:- Software.*

http://www.liv.ac.uk/~ieb/arcus.html

Aggressive Research Intelligence Facility (ARIF)

"Advancing the use of evidence on the effects of health care in the West Midlands" : ARIF is a specialist unit of three people based at the University of Birmingham, set up to help health care workers access and interpret research evidence in response to particular problems. They are a collaboration between the Department of Public Health & Epidemiology, the Department of General Practice and the Health Services Management Centre at the University and are funded for three years from 1st July 1995 by the Research and Development Department of the NHS Executive, West Midlands (see under R&D Program below). The first objective of ARIF is to provide timely access to, and advice on, existing reviews of research. *Type of resource : Organisation, Training Course Provider, Information Service.*

http://www.hsrc.org.uk/links/arif/arifhome.htm

AuRACLE

AURACLE is a co-operative research project between the Department of Information Studies at the University of Sheffield and the School of Health and Related Research (ScHARR). The aim is to develop a computer-based service capable of increasing the range of evidence-based information queries which can be handled by machine. *Type of resource : Project, WWW presence.*

http://panizzi.shef.ac.uk/auracle/aurac.html

Bandolier (ISSN : 1353-9906).

Bandolier is a newsletter produced monthly by the Anglia and Oxford NHS Region in the UK. It contains bullet points of evidence-based medicine, hence its title. The printed version is available free within the NHS and for a subscription of £30 per year (UK) and £60 overseas. *Address:-* Ann Southwell, R&D Manager (West), Anglia & Oxford Region, Tel : +44 (0) 1865 226743 Fax : +44 (0) 1865 226775).

A cumulative volume *Bandolier : the first 20 issues,* by Andrew Moore, Henry McQuay and Muir Gray was published at the end of 1995 (ISBN : 1 899137 35 1). Details from:- *Bandolier,* Pain Relief Unit, Churchill Hospital, OXFORD, Fax : +44 (0)1865 226978.

Access to *Bandolier* on the Internet is free of charge, but it may run several months behind the printed version. *Type of resource : WWW site; WWW resource list; Newsletter; Book.*
http://www.jr2.ox.ac.uk:80/Bandolier/

Best Evidence

Best Evidence on CD-ROM offers : Access to all articles from ACP Journal Club (January 1991 - December 1996); Evidence-Based Medicine (November 1995-December 1996); Updated annually with full text searching It also contains editorials about critical appraisal and clinical application of evidence and a reference glossary of statistical terms. BMA Members £33, Personal Rate £50, Institutional Rate £73. Joint rate *for Evidence-based Medicine* and *Best-Evidence* CD-Rom - 10% off CD-Rom [BMA Members £67.70, Personal Rate £99.00, Institutional Rate £151.70]. The database is also available on disk or CDROM for $98 from the Customer Service Center, American College of Physicians, Independence Mall West, Sixth Street at Race, Philadelphia, PA 19106. Tel : (800-523-1546 ext 2600) and also from the Canadian Medical Association. *Type of resource : CDROM Database, Software*

CAMS - Critical Appraisal for Medical Students

CAMS is a student-led group dedicated to provide exciting opportunities to develop the skills of applying papers to patients. For more details or to apply for membership, contact the founding members : Mark Loveland BSc *Mark.Loveland@stud.man.ac.uk ;* Robert Phillips BA *robert.phillips@somerville.ox.ac.uk;* Nicholas GN Shenker MA BM BCh *106304.1360@compuserve.com. Type of resource : World Wide Web Presence*
http://cebm.jr2.ox.ac.uk/docs/cams.html

CAT-Maker

Software developed at the Centre for Evidence Based Medicine in Oxford to produce critically appraised topics (CATs) summarising the evidence for clinicians. The software can be obtained from Douglas Badenoch at the Centre for EBM. *Type of resource:- Software.* For further details see : **http://cebm.jr2.ox.ac.uk/docs/catbank.html**

CCEPP Newsletter : The Cochrane Collaboration on Effective Professional Practice

This Newsletter is produced by the Effective Professional Practice Group and is administered by Emma Harvey, Research Fellow/Administrator, Department of Health Sciences and Clinical Evaluation, University of York, Heslington, YORK,YO1 5DD. Tel : 01904 434577, E-mail : **ccepp@york.ac.uk** (Volume 1, Number 1; May 1995) . *From Monday 5th May 1997 the CCEPP editorial base will be moving from York to the Health Services Research Unit, University of Aberdeen, Medical School, Foresterhill, Aberdeen AB9 2ZD. Type of resource : Newsletter; WWW site.* It is currently found on the Internet at : **http://hiru.mcmaster.ca/COCHRANE/newslett/**

ccinet

CCINET is an Internet discussion list, operated by the Cochrane Collaboration Informatics Project (CCIP) on behalf of the Cochrane Collaboration Informatics Working Group. It is established to facilitate communication between members of the informatics group of the CC. *Type of Resource : Discussion list.* To join this list send the command:

sub CCINET firstname lastname

as the only text of an e-mail message to:

listproc@fhs.mcmaster.ca

ccinfo

CCINFO is an Internet discussion list, operated by the Cochrane Collaboration Informatics Project (CCIP) on behalf of the Cochrane Collaboration (CC). The list is established to facilitate communication between members of the Cochrane Collaboration and rapid dissemination of : News about the Cochrane Collaboration, Announcements of new or altered information services, Announcements of Conferences, Colloquia and Meetings, Minutes of open CC meetings, Proceedings of CC Colloquia, Support for users of CC information services and listings of publications, conferences and services. *Type of Resource : Discussion list.* To join this list send the command: **sub CCINFO** firstname lastname

as the only text of an e-mail message to:

listproc@fhs.mcmaster.ca

CenterWatch Clinical Trials Listing Service

CenterWatch is a publishing company and this service provides an international listing of ongoing clinical research trials, by therapeutic area and geographic region. Headings include the clinical trials listing, profiles of the centers conducting cinical research, background information on clinical research and additional resources. There is also an email patient notification service available. *Type of resource:- WWW site*

http://www.CenterWatch.com/

Centre for Evidence Based Child Health

The newly opened Centre for Evidence-Based Child Health is part of a national network of centres for evidence-based health care. The overall aim of the Centre is to increase the provision of effective and efficient child health care through an educational programme for health professionals. Introductory seminars, short courses, MSc modules, workshops for groups in the workplace and training secondments are beng offered to paediatricians, nurses, general practitioners, healthcare purchasers and others involved in child health.

Type of resource : Organisation, Training course provider, WWW page

Address:- Dr Ruth Gilbert, 30 Guildford Street, LONDON, WC1N 1EH, Tel : +44 (0)171 242 9789, Fax : +44 (0)171 831 2823

http://www.ich.bpmf.ac.uk/ebm/ebm.htm

Centre for Evidence-Based Dentistry

Address:- Institute of Health Sciences, Anglia and Oxford RHA, Old Road, Headington, OXFORD, OX3 7LF. Tel : +44 (0) 1865 226968. *Type of Resource : Organisation, WWW presence*. The Centre is contactable via the World Wide Web at:-

http://www.bhaoral.demon.co.uk

Centre for Evidence-Based Medicine

The World Wide Web page of the Centre for Evidence-Based Medicine, established in Oxford as the first of several centres around the country whose aim broadly is to promote evidence-based health care and provide support and resources to anyone who wants to make use of them. *Address:- Centre for Evidence-based Medicine,* Level 5, John Radcliffe Hospital, Headley Way, Headington, OXFORD, OX3 9DU, Tel : +44 (0) 1865 221321. *Type of Resource : Organisation, Training Course Provider, WWW site, WWW resource list*. The Centre has a World Wide web site at:

http://cebm.jr2.ox.ac.uk

cebm-members

This mailbase discussion list functions as a discussion forum for members of the Centre for Evidence-Based Medicine. The Centre exists to promote Evidence-Based Medicine by developing educational programmes and by providing support for other Centres in the UK. This is a closed list. To apply to join send an e-mail to the list owner Douglas Badenoch at the Centre for Evidence Based Medicine (CEBM). (See the CEBM's WWW pages (above) or check the Mailbase discussion list archives for further details). *Type of resource:- Discussion list*

Centre for Evidence Based Pathology

This site, developing at the University of Nottingham, is currently a gateway to resources on EBM. However it is likely to develop into a valuable resource in its own right. *Address:-* c/o Dr David Jenkins, University of Nottingham Medical School, Histopathology Department, University Hospital, NOTTINGHAM, NG7 2UH. Tel +44 (0) 115 970 9171. Fax : +44 (0) 115 970 4852. *Type of resource:- Organisation, WWW presence, WWW resource list.*
http://www.ccc.nottingham.ac.uk/~mpzjlowe/evpath.html

Centre for Health Economics

The Centre for Health Economics (CHE) was established in 1983 and conducts research in six major areas : outcome measurement (quality of life measurement and the estimation of quality adjusted life years(QALYs), economic evaluation of alternative technologies (technology assessment), primary care, community care, and the determinants of health (other than health care). *Address:-* University of York, Heslington, YORK, YO1 5DD. *Type of resource : WWW site, WWW resource list.* The Centre has a World Wide Web site at :
http://www.york.ac.uk/inst/che/welcome.htm

Centre for Reviews and Dissemination

The NHS Centre for Reviews and Dissemination (CRD) is commissioned by the NHS Research and Development Division to produce and disseminate reviews concerning the effectiveness and cost-effectiveness of healthcare interventions. The aim is to identify and review the results of good quality health research and to disseminate actively the findings to key decision makers in the NHS and to consumers of health care services. The reviews cover the effectiveness of care for particular conditions; the effectiveness of health technologies; evidence on efficient methods of organising and delivering particular types of health care. The CRD databases are accessible over the internet and via dialup access. The first is a database of structured abstracts of good quality systematic reviews (DARE) which comment on the methodological features of published reviews and summarise the author's conclusions and any implications for health practice. The abstracts represent the end product of a detailed sifting and quality appraisal process. There is also be an economic evaluations database (NEED). The telnet address is **nhscrd.york.ac.uk** (the user ID and Password are both crduser). *Address:- Centre for Reviews and Dissemination,* University of York, Heslington, YORK, YO1 5DD. *Type of resource:- Organisation, Online Database, Information Service, Training Course Provider, WWW site*

The Centre has a World Wide Web site at:

http://www.york.ac.uk/inst/crd/welcome.htm

Clinical Effectiveness in Nursing (ISSN : 1361-9004)

This journal, to be published by Churchill Livingstone, aims to provide data on the impact of nurses' activities on clinical outcomes in all specialties. Address:- Churchill Livingstone, 1-3 Baxter's Place, Leith Walk, Edinburgh, DEH1 0BA, UK. Fax : +44 (0) 131 558 1278. *Type of resource:- Journal.*

Clinical Epidemiology Newsletter

Formerly (Volumes 1-15, 1981-1995) an occasional publication from the Department of Clinical Epidemiology and Biostatistics, McMaster University this newsletter has changed its title to the *Evidence-Based Healthcare Newsletter* (Volume 16, 1996) to reflect a growth from critical appraisal to a wider scope. It includes items on the various apects of teaching and practicing evidence based healthcare. *Type of resource:- Newsletter; WWW site.* To receive copies contact Doreen Dixon, CE&B, HSC-2C10, MUMC, 1200 Main Street West, HAMILTON, Ontario L83 3Z5. e-mail : *dixond@fhs.csu.mcmaster.ca*

(Available on McMaster Health Information Research Unit Gopher:- **gopher://hiru.csu.mcmaster.ca**).

Clinical Performance and Quality Healthcare

The official journal of the Society for Healthcare Epidemiology of America is a quarterly publication that features peer-reviewed articles that combine quality improvement strategies with clinical research. Topics include quality of health care, evidence-based medicine, outcomes research, decision analysis, the application of practice guidelines/clinical pathways and the appropriateness of care. *Address :* Clinical Performance and Quality Healthcare, 6900Grove Road, Thorofare New Jersey 08086-9864. *Type of resource : Journal*

Clinical Practice Guidelines Infobase

The clinical practice guidelines in this Canadian Medical Association collection were produced or endorsed by a national, provincial or territorial medical or health organization, professional society, government agency or expert panel. This new product is being developed in three stages. During the first stage, CMA is providing access to guidelines previously published in the Canadian Medical Association Journal (CMAJ); the guidelines to which CMAJ does not hold copyright are listed and the full text will be added when the developers have granted permission. Other guidelines will be added as they become available. *Type of resource:- WWW site*

http://www.cma.ca/cpgs/index.html

Clinical Trial Finder

A moderated list which assists individuals looking for clinical trials. *Type of resource:- Discussion List.* To join, send the email message:-

subscribe ctf firstname lastname

to *listserve@garcia.com*

Clinical Trials Mail List

An email discussion list which addresses issues related to clinical trials. *Type of resource:- Discussion List.* To join, send the email message. **subscribe MedTrial** firstname lastname

to:- *listserve@galen.imw.lublin.pl*

Clinical-Trials. Email Discussion Group

This site from PharmInfoNet describes the service available and how to join. Its purpose is to facilitate exchanges between professionals who conduct clinical trials. It addresses the techniques of performing, managing, and analyzing such trials. *Type of resource:- Discussion List*

http://pharminfo.com/conference/clntrl.html

Cochrane Collaboration

The **Cochrane Collaboration** is a group of "health care providers, consumers and scientists" who "engage in the..... collaborative enterprise of preparing, maintaining and disseminating systematic up-to-date reviews, by specialty, of all relevant randomized controlled trials (RCTs) of health care (and, when they are not available, reviews of the most reliable evidence from other sources)". Members form themselves into collaborative **Health Problem Review Groups** that carry out "exhaustive searches for all relevant trials, scrutinize these for their relevance and quality, assemble and analyze them, draw conclusions about how their net result should be applied in health care, and prepare structured reports for widespread dissemination to health care providers and planners". In addition there are **Methods Review Groups** that look at the application of methodological techniques such as economic analysis and statistical methods to the review process. All these Review Groups are coordinated by a worldwide network of **Cochrane Centres**. Currently there are Centres in Australia, Canada, Denmark (Nordic), France, Italy, Netherlands, South Africa, United States (Baltimore, San Antonio and San Francisco), as well as in the United Kingdom. The Cochrane Collaboration facilitates the creation, review, maintenance and dissemination of systematic overviews of the effects of health care. *Type of resource:- Organisation, Training Course Provider, WWW site, WWW resource list*

http://hiru.mcmaster.ca/COCHRANE/DEFAULT.HTM

This is the home page for the Collaboration and provides access to information on all its activities, to the Handbook (see next entry) as well as password-protected access to some of the reviews:

http://hiru.mcmaster.ca/COCHRANE/reviews/index.htm

and links to related sites:

http://hiru.mcmaster.ca/COCHRANE/link_0.htm

Centres

Australasian Cochrane Centre

Flinders Medical Centre, Bedford Park, SA 5042. Tel : +61 8 204 5399, Fax : +61 8 276 3305.

http://som.flinders.edu.au/fusa/cochrane/

http://wwwsom.flinders.edu.au/HTML/departments/cochranecentre/index.html

Baltimore Cochrane Center

Department of Epidemiology and Preventive Medicine, University of Maryland School of Medicine, 660 West Redwood Street, Room 133C, BALTIMORE, Maryland, USA 21201-1596. Tel +1 410 706-5295, Fax : +1 410 328-0110

Brazilian Cochrane Centre

Unidade de Meta-analise, Universidade Federal de Sao Paulo, Rua Pedro de Toledo 598 CEP 04039-001-Sao Paulo-SP BRAZIL. Tel : +55 11 570 0469, Fax : +55 11 549 2127

Canadian Cochrane Centre

Health Information Research Unit,Health Sciences Centre,McMaster University, 1200 Main Street West,HAMILTON,Ontario,Canada L8N 3Z5. Tel : +1-905-525-9140 ext 22311, Fax : +1-905-546-0401).The Canadian Cochrane Centre has a World Wide Web presence at *http://hiru.mcmaster.ca/cochrane/cochrane.htm*

Dutch Cochrane Centre

Department of Clinical Epidemiology and Biostatistics, Academic Medical Centre, University of Amsterdam Meibergdreef 15, J.2-221, Postbus 22700 1100 DE Amsterdam NETHERLANDS. Tel : +31 20 566 5602, Fax : +31 20 691 2683

French Cochrane Centre

Centre Cochrane Francais, BP 3041 (162 avenue Lacassagne), 69394 Lyon CEDEX 03, FRANCE. Tel : +33 72 11 52 50, Fax : +33 78 53 10 30

Italian Cochrane Centre

Laboratory of Clinical Epidemiology, Mario Negri Institute, Via Eritrea 62, 20157 Milano, ITALY. Tel : 39 2 39014 540, Fax : +39 2 33200 231

New England Cochrane Center

Division of Clinical Care Research, New England Medical Center, 750 Washington Street, Box 63, Boston MA 02111, USA. Tel : +1 617 636 7670, Fax : +1 617 636 8023.

Nordic Cochrane Centre

Research & Development Secretariat, Rigshospitalet, 9 Blegdamsvej, DK 2100 Copenhagen, Denmark. Tel : +45-35-45-55-71, Fax : +45-35-45-65-28

San Antonio Cochrane Center

Audie L Murphy Memorial Veterans Hospital VA ACOS/AC (11C6), 7400 Merton Minter Bouilevard, San Antonio, Texas 78284, USA. Tel : +1 210 617 5190, Fax : 1 210 617 5234

San Francisco Cochrane Centre

Institute for Health Policy Studies, University of California, 1388 Sutter Street, 11th Floor, SAN FRANCISCO, California, 94109, USA. Tel : +1 415 476 1067, Fax +1 415 476 0705

UK Cochrane Centre

Summertown Pavilion, Middle Way, OXFORD, OX2 7LG, Tel : +44 (0)1865-516300

E-mails for cochrane centres

Australasian:	cochrane@flinders.edu.au
Baltimore:	cochrane@umabnet.ab.umd.edu
Brazilian:	unifesp@epm.br
Canada:	cochrane@fhs.mcmaster.ca
Dutch:	cochrane@amc.uva.nl
French:	ccf@upcl.univ-lyon1.fr
Italian:	cochrane@imimnvx.irfmn.mnegri.it
New England:	cochrane@es.nemc.org
Nordic:	rifopg@inet.uni-c.dk
San Antonio:	cochrane@merece.uthscsa.edu
San Francisco:	sfcc@syrius.com
UK:	general@cochrane.co.uk

Cochrane Collaboration Handbook

The Cochrane Collaboration's handbook is its main working document and currently has six parts. The first section of the Handbook describes the background, aims and organisation of the Collaboration. The second, third and fourth sections are for those considering establishing review groups, field co-ordination or Cochrane centres; the fifth and sixth sections provide practical guidance (and software) for developing and maintaining registers of RCTs and Cochrane Reviews. *Type of resource:- WWW site.* The text is available on the *Cochrane Library* and at:-

http://hiru.mcmaster.ca/cochrane/handbook/default.htm

Section 1 of the Handbook is also available from a demonstration site at:-

http://synapse.uah.ualberta.ca/synapse/000n0001.htm

The complete text is available by ftp from:-

ftp.cochrane.co.uk (login anonymous, password <your e-mail address>)

ftp.hiru.mcmaster.ca (login cochrane, password archie)

The hypertext version of the Cochrane Handbook is available from the University of York ftp site:-

ftp.york.ac.uk (login anonymous, password<your e-mail address>) Files are located in /pub/users/irss31

Cochrane Collaboration on Effective Professional Practice

The Cochrane Collaboration on Effective Professional Practice is a cross-disciplinary group looking at effective interventions for changing the behaviour of health professionals. In addition to *CCEPP News* (newsletter) the group has produced a register of studies available as a read-only database via ftp. For instructions see:-

ftp://ftp.york.ac.uk/pub/users/irss31/PUB/explain.txt

The group also makes available its checklist for evaluating potential studies:-

ftp://ftp.york.ac.uk/pub/users/irss31/PUB/chkl27-3.doc

Type of resource : Software, WWW site. For further information contact:- The Cochrane Collaboration on Effective Professional Practice (CCEPP), Department of Health Sciences and Clinical Evaluation, University of York, Heslington, YORK. YO1 5DD. +44 (0)1904 434505. ***From Monday 5th May 1997 the CCEPP editorial base will be moving from York to the Health Services Research Unit, University of Aberdeen, Medical School, Foresterhill, Aberdeen AB9 2ZD.***

CCEPP's World Wide Web page is at:-

http://www.york.ac.uk/inst/ccepp/

Cochrane Database of Systematic Reviews

In addition to being part of the Cochrane Library (see below) the Cochrane Database of Systematic Reviews is published by Synapse Publishing Inc on the Internet on a subscription basis. A one year subscription costs $212.93 (Canadian Dollars) This price includes all updates to the database during the subscription period (currently four per annum). *Type of resource:- WWW database* See the Synapse Publishing Home Page at:-

http://www.wepublish.com/jmb/default.htm

Cochrane Library.

A disk/CD-ROM database containing four databases : The Cochrane Database of Systematic Reviews (CDSR), the York Database of Abstracts of Reviews of Effectiveness (DARE), the Cochrane Controlled Trials Register (CCTR) and the Cochrane Review Methodology Database (CRMD). Version 3 also contains the Cochrane Collaboration Handbook, details of all Cochrane entities and the ScHARR Netting the Evidence Guide to EBP sources on the Internet. Available for £95 (personal) or £120 (institutional) plus VAT, updated quarterly, from British Medical Journal Publishing Group, PO Box 295, London WC1H 9TE (0171 383 6185). The Cochrane Database of Systematic Reviews is also being marketed over the Internet by Synapse Publishing Inc. (See Cochrane Collaboration Newsletter, October 1996 page 1 for further details). *Type of resource:- CDROM Database; Software*

Cochrane Library Training Guide

This training guide produced by Anglia and Oxford Region R&D Directorate is aimed at librarians and other end-users of the Cochrane Library either as a self-training guide, materials for an in-house course or as end-user documentation. The guide includes an introduction on the value of systematic reviews and the work of the Cochrane Collaboration and NHS Centre for Reviews and Dissemination. It also contains a pictorial guide to the databases on the Library with simple exercises to encourage the user to explore its features. It includes model answers and is accompanied by a Powerpoint slide presentation. *Type of resource:- Training materials*

http://libsun1.jr2.ox.ac.uk/nhserdd/aordd/new.htm

Cochrane News : The Cochrane Collaboration Newsletter

This Newsletter is produced by the Australasian Cochrane Centre. *Type of resource : Newsletter; WWW site.* Two issues have been published to date and both are available on the World Wide Web at:-

http://hiru.mcmaster.ca/cochrane/news.htm and

http://hiru.mcmaster.ca/cochrane/default.htm

Cochrane Pregnancy and Childbirth Database.

[Note : The original product of the Cochrane Collaboration, this disk/CDROM is no longer available as a separate database. The systematic reviews of interventions in pregnancy and childbirth are now incorporated in the Cochrane Library (see above). The complete text of "A Guide to Effective Care in Pregnancy and Childbirth (2nd edition) is available in two volumes from Oxford University Press. Type of resource:- Book; CDROM Database; Software].

Controlled Clinical Trials incorporating Clinical Trials & Metaanalysis (ISSN : 0197-2456)

Controlled Clinical Trials is a source of current information on the design, methods, and operational aspects of controlled clinical trials and follow-up studies. Each monthly issue highlights unusual design features of specific trials or follow-up studies that provide readers with workable solutions to operational, methodological, legal, and ethical problems associated with clinical trials. The journal is published by Elsevier Science and further details are available from:-

http://www.elsevier.nl:80/inca/publications/store/5/0/5/7/5/8/

Type of resource : Journal

Critical Appraisal Skills Programme (CASP)

CASP is a UK project that aims to help health service decision makers develop skills in the critical appraisal of evidence about effectiveness, in order to promote the delivery of evidence-based health care. At the heart of CASP's work is a cascade of half day workshops that introduce participants to the key skills needed to find and make sense of evidence to support health service decisions. CASP introduces people to the ideas of evidence-based medicine and, through critical appraisal of systematic reviews, to the related ideas of the Cochrane Collaboration. *Address:- Critical Appraisal Skills Programme,* Claire Spittlehouse, Institute of Health Sciences, Anglia and Oxford RHA, Old Road, Headington, OXFORD, OX3 7LF, Tel : +44 (0)1865 226968; Fax : +44 (0)1865 226775. *Type of resource:- Organisation, Training provider, WWW presence*

http://fester.his.path.cam.ac.uk/phealth/casphome.htm

Filocasp

This Idealist-based software package provides details of articles suitable for critical appraisal together with scenarios, checklists, crib sheets and other supportive materials. Contact CASP for further details. *Type of resource:- Software, Training materials.*

Department of Health

The Director of Research and Development is responsible for advising the Secretary of State for Health across the range of his responsibilities and interests in research. These include the National Health Service (NHS) research and development programme, the Department's policy research programme and the health research of the non-departmental public bodies, the Concordat between the health departments and the Medical Research Council (MRC), the relationships with other research councils, the medical charities and industry, and the interface with the health-related R&D of other government departments and the European Community (EC). An information pack, with details of the NHS programme, the Department's policy research programme and wider research issues, is available on request from : Office of the Director of Research and Development, Department of Health, Richmond House, 79 Whitehall, London, SW1A 2NS. Fax 0171 210 5868 or by downloading the full text of the information pack as a zip file (68k). *Type of resource:- Organisation, WWW site*

http://www.open.gov.uk/doh/rdd1.htm

Development and Evaluation Committee Reports (DEC Reports)

These reports have been prepared as part of the Development and Evaluation Service funded by the Research and Development Directorate South and West. They are intended to provide rapid, accurate and usable information on health technology effectiveness to purchasers, clinicians, managers and researchers in the South and West. *Type of resource:- WWW site*

http://cochrane.epi.bris.ac.uk/rd/publicat/dec/intro.htm

DHSS-Data

The database of the Department of Health (formerly Department of Health and Social Security) contains bibliographic records for articles on the quality of care together with nationally-produced guidelines and policy statements. (Available via Datastar, Knight-Ridder Information, London). *Type of resource:- Online Database*

Disease Management and Health Outcomes

A monthly journal designed as a forum for collating, evaluating and disseminating practical knowledge on the application of components of disease management based on best evidence. The journal incorporates outcomes research into outcomes measurement and management programs and aims to assist in the preliminary communication of programmes. Contact ADIS International offices in Chester (UK), Langhorne PA (US) or Hong Kong. *Type of resource:- Journal, Web presence*

http://www.adis.com

EBM Searching Tutorial

For those interested in searching skills in an Evidence Based Medicine environment, this is an interactive tutorial guiding the user through steps in query formulation and searching. *Type of resource:- Computer Assisted Learning*

http://jeffline.tju.edu/CWIS/OAC/informatics/activities/ebm_info.html

Effective Health Care (ISSN: 0965-0288).

Eight bulletins per year available on subscription from : Churchill Livingstone, 102-108 Clerkenwell Road, LONDON, EC1M 5SA. Tel : +44 (0)171 282 8303, Fax : +44 (0)171282 8311. (See articles : by Torgerson, Ryan & Donaldson. Effective Health Care Bulletins : are they efficient? *Quality in Health Care* 1995; 4 : 48-51 and Sheldon, Long, Freemantle & Song. The ideal : enemy of the useful? *Quality in Health Care* 1995; 4 : 52-54. *Type of Resource:- Bulletin*

Effectiveness Matters.

Periodic bulletins published by the NHS Centre for Reviews and Dissemination. Tel : 01904 433 634, Fax : 01904 433661, E-mail revdis@york.ac.uk. Issue 1; April 1995 entitled Aspirin and Myocardial infarction, Issue 2, September 1995 entitled Helicobacter Pylori and Peptic Ulcer, Volume 2 Issue 1 - October 1996 entitled Influenza Vaccination and Older People. Volume 2 Issue 2 - February 1997 entitled Screening for Prostate Cancer. *Type of resource:- Bulletin*

EQUIP Magazine

EQUIP is an organisation which is responsible for the education of general practitioners and their staff in North Essex. This page gives audits by subject (e.g. asthma, diabetes), newsletters, educational events and other information.

http://www.equip.ac.uk/

EMBASE

Produced by Excerpta Medica this database complements MEDLINE with its coverage of European Literature and is particularly strong in pharmacology. Overlap with MEDLINE has been estimated at about 35%. (Available via Datastar, Knight-Ridder Information, London and via BIDS on the Joint Academic Network JANet). *Type of resource:- Online Database*

European Congress of the Internet in Medicine, October 14-17, 1996.

This conference contains several papers of interest to evidence based practitioners, including:-

Badenoch D. CATmaker : Critical Appraisal Tools on the Web
http://www.mednet.org.uk/mednet/ep4.htm

Glanville J and Smith I. Evaluating the Options for Developing Databases to Support Research-Based Medicine at the NHS Centre for Reviews and Dissemination
http://www.mednet.org.uk/mednet/am3.htm

Kelly MA and Oldham J. The Internet and Randomised Controlled Trials
http://www.mednet.org.uk/mednet/ca16.htm

Evidence-based Cardiovascular Medicine (ISSN : 1361-2611)

Quarterly journal from Churchill Livingstone that provides summaries of high quality articles alongside related commentaries on all aspects of cardiovascular medicine. The journal is split into two sections; the first presents summaries of key articles whilst the second contains educational articles on aspects of evidence based practice. Contact Churchill Livingstone on +44 (0) 171 282 8303 (Phone) or +44 (0) 171 282 8311 (Fax) or *louisea@pearson-pro.com* (Email). *Type of resource:- Journal*

Evidence based Health Policy and Management (ISSN : 1363-4038)

Edited by JA Muir-Gray this quarterly journal from Churchill Livingstone that provides summaries of high quality articles alongside related commentaries on all aspects of cardiovascular medicine. The journal is split into two sections; the first presents summaries of key articles whilst the second contains educational articles on aspects of evidence based practice. Contact Churchill Livingstone on +44 (0) 171 282 8303 (Phone) or +44 (0) 171 282 8311 (Fax) or *louisea@pearson-pro.com* (Email). *Type of resource:- Journal*

evidence-based-health

Evidence based health (EBH) is the application of critical appraisal to problems in health care. This list is for teachers and practitioners in health related fields; to announce meetings and courses; stimulate discussion; air controversies and aid the implementation of EBH. *Type of resource : Discussion list.*

To join this list send the command:

join evidence-based-health firstname lastname

as the only text of an e-mail message to:

mailbase@mailbase.ac.uk

Evidence based Healthcare Links Pages

A number of sites have set up pages of links to Evidence Based Resources. These are good starting points for listings to update this guide. *Type of resource : WWW resource list.* Examples are:-

Cambridge University Public Health
http://fester.his.path.cam.ac.uk/phealth/phweb.html

Centre for Evidence Based Medicine
http://cebm.jr2.ox.ac.uk/docs/otherebmgen.html

Evidence Based Medicine : New York Academy of Medicine
http://library.nyam.org/library/eblinks.html

Evidence Based Medicine (Norway)
http://rhpc205.uio.no/ebm.html

Health Promotion Research Internet Network
http://www.dsg.ki.se/phm/hprin/main.html

Introduction to Evidence Based Medicine (Australia) includes Australian mirror of Netting the Evidence guide [see below]
http://www.health.su.oz.au/resource/ebm1196a.htm

McMaster University, Canada
http://hiru.hirunet.mcmaster.ca/ebm/

Oxford Clinical Information WWW Pages
http://sable.ox.ac.uk/~clnguidc/world.htm

South and West Health Care Libraries
http://cochrane.epi.bris.ac.uk/rd/links/ebm.htm

Evidence Based Journals

In addition to the generic *Evidence Based Medicine* journal published by BMJ Publishing (see below) there is a whole series of titles planned by Churchill Livingstone. For further information contact : Mark Lane, Managing Editor, Healthcare Information and Management, Churchill Livingstone, 102-108 Clerkenwell Road, LONDON EC1M 5SA. Tel : +44 (0)171 282 8304, Fax : +44 (0)171 282 8311. *email : markl@pearson-pro-com* The first two titles are due to appear in 1997:-

Evidence Based Cardiovascular Medicine (ISSN : 1361-2611) Edited by Salim Yusuf

Evidence Based Health Policy and Management (ISSN : 1363-4038) Edited by JA Muir-Gray.

Additional titles planned include:-

Evidence Based Gastroenterology (ISSN : 1361-262X)

Evidence Based Infectious Diseases (ISSN : 1364-3088)

Evidence Based Musculoskeletal Medicine (ISSN : 1364-3096)

Evidence Based Neurology (ISSN : 1363-4046)

Evidence Based Obstetrics and Gynecology (ISSN : 1361-259X)

Evidence Based Oncology (ISSN : 1363-4054)

Evidence Based Pain Management (ISSN : 1361-2581)

Evidence Based Pediatrics and Child Health (1363-4062)

Evidence Based Respiratory Medicine (ISSN : 1364-307X)

Evidence Based Surgery (ISSN : 1361-2603)

Evidence Based Medicine

The purpose of *Evidence-Based Medicine* is to alert clinicians to important advances in internal medicine, general and family practice, surgery, psychiatry, paediatrics, and obstetrics and gynaecology by selecting from the biomedical literature those original and review articles whose results are most likely to be both true and useful. These articles are summarised in value-added abstracts and commented on by clinical experts. Published by the BMJ Publishing Group [ISSN : 1357 5376]. Publication : Bimonthly. Subscription Rates : Institutional £54, Personal £38 BMA members £38, BMA student members £16. *Type of resource:- Journal, WWW site*

http://www.acponline.org/journals/ebm/ebmmenu.htm

http://www.bmjpg.com/data/ebm.htm

Evidence Based Medicine Resource List

This site maintained by Chris Cox at the Library at the University of Hertfordshire has useful references and links to other resources. This is probably the best single compilation page on EBM on the Web. *Type of resource : WWW resource list.*

http://www.herts.ac.uk/lrc/subjects/health/ebm.htm

Evidence Based Nursing (ISSN : 1367-6539)

The future appearance of this journal was announced in March 1997. It will begin in September 1997 and a pilot issue is available. For further details contact:- Nursing Standard, Viking House 17-19 Peterborough Rd, Harrow on the Hill, Middlesex HA1 2AX, UK. Tel (44) 181 423 1066 (0181 423 1066 in the UK), Fax (44) 181 423 3867 (0181 423 3867 in the UK). *Type of resource : Journal*

Evidence Based Purchasing

Evidence-Based Purchasing is a bi-monthly digest of evidence about effective care and is intended to support the commissioning role. It is a selection of material received, commissioned, or found in journals by South and West R&D Directorate. Available from:- Ben Toth, Information & Communications Co-ordinator, Research & Development Directorate, Canynge Hall, Whiteladies Road, BRISTOL, BS8 2PR. Tel : +44 (0) 117 928 7224 (Email : Ben.Toth@bristol.ac.uk). Issues of *Evidence-Based Purchasing* have been added to the Internet. *Type of resource : Newsletter, WWW site*

http://cochrane.epi.bris.ac.uk/rd/publicat/ebpurch/index.htm

Evidence Based Topics

A list of EBM topics organised alphabetically by Medical Subject Heading (MeSH) with hypertext links to the relevant WWW page. Amongst the sources covered are Bandolier, some of the EBM journal clubs on the internet, the AHCPR and US and Canadian Preventative Task Force Guidelines. One can follow up a MEDLINE search by looking at the appropriate MeSH heading in this very useful list. *Type of resource : WWW resource list*

http://www.ohsu.edu/bicc-informatics/ebm/ebm_topics.htm

Framework for Appropriate Care Throughout Sheffield

Address:- Rosalind Eve, Project Director - FACTS, University of Sheffield, Regent Court, 30 Regent Street, SHEFFIELD, S1 4DA, Tel : +44 (0) 114 282 5658 Fax : +44 (0) 114 275 5763. E-mail : facts@sheffield.ac.uk. *Type of resource : Organisation, WWW presence*

http://www.shef.ac.uk/uni/projects/facts

Finding the Evidence Workshop

These workshops were developed by the Health Libraries and Information Network (HeLIN) in Anglia and Oxford Region as a follow-on workshop for people who had previously attended a critical appraisal (CASP) workshop. Workshop organiser packs are available from the address given below. *Address:-* The Health Care Libraries Unit, Oxford Radcliffe Hospital, The John Radcliffe, OXFORD OX3 9DU. Tel:- +44 (0) 1865 221951, Fax:- +44 (0) 1865 220040.

gp-uk

GP-UK facilitates discussion on new ideas, research, workshops, seminars, conferences, grants, education, software development etc for the UK General Practice (Family Medicine) community. Non-UK views are also welcome. GP-UK intends to promote collaborative work, problem solving and support. *Type of resource : Discussion list.*

To join this list send the command:

join gp-uk firstname lastname

as the only text of an e-mail message to:

mailbase@mailbase.ac.uk

Getting Easier Access to Reviews

This Idealist mini reference database for purchasers contains details of reviews identified from MEDLINE, from the academic grey literature and from UK professional bodies. GEARS is an IT database of services of importance to Health Commissions It is produced by the Wessex Institute for Health Research and Development (see below). *Type of resource : Software*

Guide to Clinical Preventive Services

The entire text of the commercially published version of the 1989 report of the U.S. Preventive Services Task Force, the Guide to Clinical Preventive Services:

http://cpmcnet.columbia.edu/health.sci/.gcps/gcps000.html

This influential publication attempts to systematically assess the effectiveness of numerous screening interventions. *Type of resource : Book, WWW site.* It is also available in print form:- U.S. Preventive Services Task Force. *Guide to Clinical Preventive Services.* Baltimore : Williams and Wilkins; 1996.

Health Economics Research Group (HERG)

HERG aims to undertake high quality, policy relevant research and to contribute to the development of evaluation methodologies. The current research programme has a unifying focus on economic evaluation of health technologies. *Address:-* Brunel University, Uxbridge, Middlesex, UB8 3PH. Tel : +44 (0) 1895 203331. *Type of resource:- Organisation, WWW site, Training provider*

http://http3.brunel.ac.uk:8080/depts/herg/home.html

health-econeval

This list will facilitate economic evaluation of health services and health care interventions; support the Cochrane Collaboration in using economic information in systematic reviews; share experience and information on cost-effectiveness; produce a regular newsletter. All are welcome. *Type of resource : Discussion list.*

To join this list send the command:

join health-econeval firstname lastname

as the only text of an e-mail message to:

mailbase@mailbase.ac.uk

Health Information Research Unit (HIRU)

The Health Information Research Unit is a useful first stopping place for evidence-based practice. It provides a "Quicklist" which includes Preventive Care Guidelines 1991, Guide to Clinical Preventive Services, Computers for Patient Education, Clinical Informatics Network Home Page (CLINT) and Structured Abstracts of Clinical Practice Guidelines. *Type of resource:- Organisation, Training Course Provider, WWW resource list, WWW site .* The location is:- **http://hiru.mcmaster.ca/fast.htm**

A special evidence based health care resource has been set up at:

http://hiru.mcmaster.ca/ebm/default.htm

Projects associated with HIRU - McMaster include:-

Clinical Informatics Network (CLINT)

The goal of the Clinical Informatics Network (CLINT) is to enable the teaching and practice of evidence-based care and thereby to facilitate improved patient care and health outcomes. We have developed software systems with innovations in clinician-computer interaction, evidence-based health information resources, and automated collection of data about how users interact with information resources. The CLINT system can be used as a laboratory for health informatics experiments. *Type of resource : Project*

Clinical Practice Enhancement Project (CPEP)

The Clinical Practice Enhancement Project (CPEP) endeavors to ease implementation of clinical practice guidelines through the development, evaluation, and dissemination of clinical information tools, with emphasis on the collection, analysis and application of patient-reported health data. Custom hardware and software for patient-computer interaction and guideline-based clinician reminders are described. *Type of resource : Project*

The Guidelines Appraisal Project (GAP)

The Guidelines Appraisal Project (GAP) helps health services researchers, policy makers, and practitioners appraise, select, summarize and disseminate information about clinical practice guidelines. Its Internet services include results of national surveys, guides for appraising and abstracting guidelines and a growing database of structured abstracts of clinical practice guidelines. *Type of resource : Project*

http://hiru.mcmaster.ca/cpg/default.htm

Heal-Net/RE-LAIS

HEALNet/RELAIS is a multidisciplinary research initiative that partners academia, government, and industry across Canada to improve the health of Canadians, productivity in the workplace, and the efficiency of the health care system to benefit Canada's global economic development. This Networks of Centres of Excellence initiative maintains internet services to facilitate communication among network members and to showcase research and development projects sponsored by Heal-Net. *Type of resource : Project*

Health Information Resource Executive (HIREX)

The Health Information Resource Executive is a software system for Microsoft Windows and for Internet that allows health organizations to build, manage and disseminate inventories of items (people, groups, organizations, projects), their relationships, and their products (conventional or internet publications). *Type of resource : Software*

The Ontario Health Care Evaluation Network (OHCEN)

The mission of the Ontario Health Care Evaluation Network (OHCEN) is to build partnerships among researchers and decision makers, enhance health care research in Ontario, ensure its relevance to health care problems, improve the accessibility of research evidence to decision makers and encourage the application of research evidence to health care decisions for the benefit of the public. Its Internet service introduces the network and features a growing inventory of health service researchers, projects and internet products in Ontario. *Type of resource : Project*

Health-Pro

Listserver specifically for Clinical Practice Guidelines. On **Health-Pro**, discussions of Practice Guidelines take place with input from around the world. A group of frontline working physicians and nurses has started building sets of Foresighted Practice Guidelines for use at the patient encounter. *Type of resource : Discussion list, WWW site.* To join the practice guidelines listserver send an e-mail to:-

listserv@netcom.com

Subject : Practice Guidelines

with, in the body of the text:-

subscribe health-pro

Also see the Practice Guidelines Web site:-

http://members.aol.com/sigalg3958/mypage.html

HEALTHSTAR

(Available via Silverplatter. Formerly HEALTHPLAN, from 1996 onwards this CD-ROM also includes the contents of the HSTAR database. [See article by Bronson RJ. Health Services Technology Assessment Research (HSTAR) : an introduction. *Medical Reference Services Quarterly* 1994 Winter; 13 (4) : 35-43]. (Contact National Library of Medicine, Bethesda, US [e-mail; mms@nlm.nih.gov for access or nichs@nlm.nih.gov for content.). *Type of resource:- Online database, CD-ROM Database*

Health Technology Assessment Reports

Address: The Programme Manager, National Coordinating Centre for Health Technology Assessment, Dawn House, Romsey Road, WINCHESTER, SO22 5DH. The reports of the NHS Health Technology Assessment Programme are listed at this site. Full reports can be purchased from the above address and executive summaries are available free of charge. Executive summaries can also be viewed by clicking on the hypertext links. *Type of resource: WWW Presence*

http://www.soton.ac.uk/~wi/hta/htapubs.html

IFMH Inform - IFM Healthcare Newsletter

(Information for the Management of Health Care) (Triennial). Bruce Madge, Head of the Health Care Information Service, The British Library, 25 Southampton Buildings, LONDON, WC2A 1AW. Tel : +44 (0) 171 412 7933 Fax : +44 (0) 171 412 7984. e-mail : bruce.madge@bl.uk. *Type of resource:- Newsletter.*

Institute of Health Sciences (Oxford)

This site states its intention to provide an Evidence-Based Healthcare Toolbox to complement the publication of the book *Evidence-Based Healthcare* (Churchill Livingstone) and thus update its contents. *Type of resource:- Organisation, Training Course Provider, WWW presence, (to become WWW site):-*

http://info.ox.ac.uk/~ihsinfo/ebh.html

Institute for Clinical Evaluative Sciences

The Institute for Clinical Evaluative Sciences in Ontario (ICES) is a non-profit research organization dedicated to conducting research that contributes to the effectiveness, quality and efficiency of health care in the province of Ontario. *Type of resource:- Organisation, Information Service, WWW presence.* It produces the newsletter for physicians:-

informed. (ISSN : 1201-2475)

Informed Address:- Institute of Clinical Evaluative Sciences, G-106, 2075 Bayview Avenue, Toronto, ON M4N 3M5, Canada Tel : (41) 480-6747. *Type of resource:- Bulletin*
http://www.ices.on.ca/

Introduction to Evidence Based Medicine

This site provided by the Clinical Audit department at South Buckinghamshire NHS Trust succinctly summarises the main principles of Evidence Based Medicine. *Type of resource : WWW presence.*

http://www.wghaudit.demon.co.uk/aud6.html

Journal Club on the Web

This web site is an experiment in implementing an on-line, interactive general medical "journal club" which periodically summarizes and critiques articles from the recent medical literature and collects and posts readers' comments.The articles are primarily in the field of adult internal medicine, and mainly from the NEJM, Annals of Internal Medicine, JAMA and the Lancet. *Type of resource : WWW site*

http://www.journalclub.org/

Journal of Clinical Effectiveness (ISSN : 1361-5874)

A quarterly multidisciplinary journal, previously published as *Medical Audit News*, that addresses the linked concepts of evidence based practice, clinical effectiveness, guidelines and clinical audit. Contact Churchill Livingstone on +44 (0) 171 282 8303 (Phone) or +44 (0) 171 282 8311 (Fax) or *louisea@pearson-pro.com* (Email). *Type of resource:- Journal*

Journal of Clinical Epidemiology (ISSN : 0895 4356)

Published monthly by Elsevier Science, the *Journal of Clinical Epidemiology* aims to provide timely, authoritative studies developed from the interplay of clinical medicine, epidemiology, biostatistics and pharmacoepidemiology. Articles are oriented toward methodology, clinical research or both. A special section, *Pharmacoepidemiology Reports*, is dedicated to the rapid publication of articles on the clinical epidemiologic investigation of pharmaceutical agents.*Type of resource:- Journal.* Further details from:-

http://www.elsevier.nl:80/inca/publications/store/5/2/5/4/7/2/

Journal of Evaluation in Clinical Practice (ISSN : 1365-2753)

The *Journal of Evaluation and Clinical Practice,* published by Blackwell Science, aims to promote critical inquiry into clinical practice within Medicine, Nursing and the healthcare professions. All aspects of clinical practice evaluation are of interest to the Journal, particularly those which examine the dimensions of effectiveness, appropriateness and efficiency in clinical care. *Type of resource:- Journal*

Further details from:-

http://www.blacksci.co.uk/products/journals/jecp.htm

Journal of Family Practice Journal Club Web Page

The JFP Journal Club is a feature of the Journal of Family Practice which each month reviews 7-10 important articles from the primary care literature. The goal is to identify articles which have the potential to change the way you practice, critically appraise them, and make specific recommendations for clinical practice (called POEM's, for Patient Oriented Evidence That Matters). The editors review some 80 clinical journals every month covering the most important findings for family physicians in the medical literature on a timely basis. A valuable feature is the provision for e-mail discussion and debate of the issues around individual articles. *Type of resource : WWW site, Journal*

http://www.phymac.med.wayne.edu/jfp/jclub.htm

Journal of Health Services Research and Policy (ISSN : 1355-8196)

This quarterly journal examines health services research and policy, and their inter-relationship, in order to bridge the gap between them and to confront and resolve the various dilemmas faced by practitioners, managers and politicians. Contact Churchill Livingstone on +44 (0) 171 282 8303 (Phone) or +44 (0) 171 282 8311 (Fax) or *louisea@pearson-pro.com* (Email). *Type of resource:- Journal*

Journal of Quality in Clinical Practice (ISSN : 1320-5455)

The quarterly *Journal of Quality in Clinical Practice* aims to provide a forum to facilitate the work of those with an interest in quality in healthcare primarily addressing the factual reporting of peer review activity within hospitals and healthcare institutions. The Journal informs readers of health policies and examines processes of health care, by publishing original articles, abstracts, news and comments on clinical review meetings, and developments. *Type of resource:- Journal.* Contact Blackwell Science or access the Blackwell Science Web site:-

http://www.blacksci.co.uk/products/journals/xjqcp.htm

lis-medical

This list, though primarily intended for medical and health care librarians, has recently proved an important source for identifying evidence based practice materials. A regular feature is a weekly digest from the US-based MEDLIB list where there have been several postings on the Cochrane Collaboration and locations for several resources on effectiveness of healthcare.

Type of resource : Discussion list

To join this list send the command:

join lis-medical firstname lastname

as the only text of an e-mail message to:

mailbase@mailbase.ac.uk

Literature Searching (using methodological filters)

A number of sites offer assistance in filtering out higher quality articles from databases, such as MEDLINE, based on methodological terms found in either the abstracts or subject indexing:. *Type of resource:- WWW site*

Search strategy to identify reviews and meta-analyses in Medline and CINAHL (NHS CRD)

http://www.york.ac.uk/inst/crd/search.htm

Evidence-based Medicine (EBM) and MEDLINE searches (Charing Cross Medical Library)

http://s1.cxwms.ac.uk/School/Library/ebh.html

Evidence-based Medicine (EBM) and MEDLINE (OVID) by Reinhard Wentz (North Thames Regional Library and Information Unit)

http://www.nthames.tpdme.ac.uk/strategi.htm

Filtering your literature search results (University of Rochester)

http://www.urmc.rochester.edu/smd/Medicine/imclerk/filterhandout.html

Hints for Diagnosis and Therapy Searches on MEDLINE (University of Rochester)

http://www.urmc.rochester.edu/smd/Medicine/imclerk/morehints.html

How to search for clinical practice guidelines (McMaster)

http://hiru.hirunet.mcmaster.ca/ebm/userguid/8_lit.htm

Searching for the best evidence in clinical journals (Centre for EBM)

http://cebm.jr2.ox.ac.uk/docs/searching html

Master's Programme in Evidence-Based Health Care

Oxford University's Centre for Continuing Professional Development offers a part-time Postgraduate Certificate/Postgraduate Diploma/Masters of Science in Evidence-Based Health Care. Information is available from Elaine Welsh or Venetia Hill-Perkins - tel. +44 (0)1865 280347/270310, fax +44 (0)1865 270386, email *elaine.welsh@conted.ox.ac.uk* or *venetia.hill-perkins@conted.ox.ac.uk*

MD Digests

This feature of the Physician's Page of the Silverplatter information resource includes clinical questions answered from a recent article of literature and supported by a selective bibliography. *Type of Resource:- WWW site*

http://php2.silverplatter.com/physicians/digest.htm

MEDLINE

The primary source of biomedical bibliographic information. Details on harnessing its full potential can be found under the **Literature Searching** section (Available via Datastar, Knight-Ridder Information, London; British Library; U.S. National Library of Medicine; Silverplatter; CD-Plus (Ovid) and various complimentary or subscription-based services on the Internet). *Type of Resource:- CD-ROM Database, Online database, WWW database*

The National Coordinating Centre for Health Technology Assessment (NCCHTA)

Address: The Programme Manager, NCCHTA, Dawn House, Romsey Road, WINCHESTER, SO22 5DH. On the 1st June 1996 the National Coordinating Centre for Health Technology Assessment was established to take responsibility for managing, providing support to, developing and promulgating the HTA programme as a whole.

The NCCHTA represents a collaboration between the Wessex Institute for Health Research and Development at the University of Southampton and the University of York's Centre for Health Economics and Department of Health Sciences and Clinical Evaluation. In addition, the NHS Centre for Reviews and Dissemination also at the University of York provides information support on a contractual basis. *Type of resource: WWW site*

http://www.soton.ac.uk/~wi/hta/index.html

National Institutes for Health (NIH) Consensus Program Information Service

Provides official statements developed by experts participating in NIH's medical technology assessment and transfer program. Recent subjects have included total hip replacement, optimal calcium intake, ovarian cancer, effect of corticosteroids for fetal maturation, helicobacter pylori in peptic ulcer disease and morbidity and mortality of dialysis. *Type of Resource:- WWW site*

Gopher

gopher://gopher.nih.gov/Health and Clinical Information

ftp

ftp://public.nlm.nih.gov/hstat/nihcdcs

For details of the World Wide Web service see the following entry:-

The National Library of Medicine's Health Services/Technology Assessment Text (HSTAT)

This WWW resource contains the following collections AHCPR Supported Guidelines, AHCPR Technology Assessments and Reviews, ATIS (HIV/AIDS Technical Information), Warren G. Magnuson Clinical Research Studies {see below}, NIH Consensus Development Program, PHS Guide to Clinical Preventive Services (1989) and SAMHSA/CSAT Treatment Improvement Protocol (TIP). *Type of resource : WWW database*

http://text.nlm.nih.gov/ftrs/gateway

Netting the Evidence -

A ScHARR Introduction to Evidence Based Practice on the Internet, the World Wide Web based equivalent of this printed resource list. *Type of resource : WWW resource list*

http://www.shef.ac.uk/uni/academic/R-Z/scharr/ir/netting.html

Nuffield Institute for Health

Address:- 71-75 Clarendon Road, LEEDS, LS2 9LP. Tel : +44 (0) 113 233 6966, Fax : +44 (0) 113 246 0899. *Type of Resource : Organisation, Information Provider, WWW site*

HELMIS

The database of the Nuffield Institute of Health is particularly strong on British quality and management issues. Available on subscription. Contact : Information Resources Centre at the address shown above. *Type of resource:- Online database.*

Office of Health Economics

A drug industry funded organisation that provides information on economic aspects of healthcare. As well as an extensive publications programme and the *OHE News* newsletter the organisation has produced a new specialised data service, in collaboration with the International Federation of Pharmaceutical Manufacturers Associations, known as HEED (a Health Economic Evaluations Database). This CD-ROM-based database contains information on health economics articles, in particular studies of cost-effectiveness (and other forms of economic evaluation) with objective analysis of key articles. HEED now has more than 6,000 bibliographic references and 2,200 reviewed articles, building up through monthly updates to contain a comprehensive bibliography of all published economic literature. For further information on the OHE-IFPMA database contact : Gerry Crosbie, Project Manager, OHE-IFPMA Database Limited, 12 Whitehall, LONDON SW1A 2DY. *Tel* : +44 (0)171 930 3477 ext. 1474 or *Fax :* +44 (0)171 747 1419.

http://www.abpi.org.uk/ohe.htm

Office of Technology Assessment

Although the remit of the U.S. based Office of Technology Assessment is much broader than just healthcare they do produce a number of useful reports; including the report "Identifying Health Technologies that Work". *Type of resource:- Organisation, WWW site.* The full text of their reports is available from this site.

http://www.wws.princeton.edu:80/~ota/

Online Journal of Current Clinical Trials

The *Online Journal of Current Clinical Trials* offers peer-reviewed, primary medical research, reviews, meta-analyses, methodological papers, and editorials. Published by Chapman & Hall, it includes information on trials or therapies, procedures, and other interventions relevant to care in all fields of medicine and allied health. Type of resource:- *CD-ROM database, WWW database, WWW presence :* Details of this can be obtained from OCLC Journals (Distributors) at:-

http://www.oclc.org/oclc/promo/ejo_list.htm#cct

 or Chapman and Hall (Publishers) at:-

http://www.thomson.com/chaphall/cct.html

Pocket Card : How to use an Article about.......

These guides, adapted from pocket cards developed for the Teaching Evidence Based Medicine Workshops, are designed as checklists for evaluating different types of article. They include useful aide-memoires for calculating clinically significant measures together with best single searching strategies for retrieving different types of article. *Type of resource:- WWW site*

Therapy

http://hiru.hirunet.mcmaster.ca/ebm/userguid/2_ther_p.htm

Another source for these checklists, also available as cards in the *Evidence Based Medicine* book by David Sackett, is the **Medicine On-Line** site at:-

http://www.priory.co.uk/journals/med/danny.htm

Practice Guidelines : mental health

Contains details of guidelines and practice parameters for many of the American professional organisations. Contact:- Marian Benjamin at:- **webmaster@mhsource.com**. *Type of resource:- WWW site.*

http://www.mhsource.com

Prescrire International (ISSN: 1167-7422)

This journal is a bi-monthly English selection of articles from the monthly French-Language journal *La revue Prescrire*. It contains comprehensive evaluations of major new drugs and indications, together with reviews of adverse effects and therapeutic strategies. *Address:-* Prescrire International, BP 459, 75527 Paris CEDEX 11, FRANCE. Tel : +33 1 47 00 94 45, Fax : +33 1 48 07 87 32. *Type of resource:- Journal*

Primary Care Evidence-Based Medicine Topics.

This is an alphabetical list of MeSH terms of evidence-based medicine topics of interest to primary care physicians. Documents in this list either show some evidence of a systematic review of the literature or critical appraisal of an article or articles. *Type of resource : Internet Resource*

http://www.ohsu.edu/bicc-informatics/ebm/ebm_topics.htm

PRISE : Primary Care Sharing the Evidence

The PRISE project, based in the Institute of Health Sciences in Oxford, is supported by the Anglia and Oxford R&D Directorate and is part of a development programme managed by the Health Care Libraries Unit. It focuses on twelve Primary Health care sites and aims to provide access to good quality information for GPs and other practice-based professionals. The index also includes primary care links, evidence-based medicine and research projects. The University of East Anglia and the North West Anglia Health Authority are collaborating in a complementary project based in Anglia called PRIMA (Primary Care Information Management across Anglia) will be starting soon. *Type of resource : Project, WWW site, WWW resource list*

http://wwwlib.jr2.ox.ac.uk/prise/prise.html

Promoting Action on Clinical Effectiveness (PACE)

The PACE initiative arose from GRiPP and FACTS to "create a network of projects to demonstrate the effective implementation of evidence based practice and to identify the factors for success". *Address:-* Project Manager (Mr Michael Dunning), King's Fund Development Centre, 11-13 Cavendish Square, LONDON, W1M 0AN. Tel : +44 (0)171 307 2400, Fax : +44 (0)171 307 2801. *Type of resource:- Project, Newsletter, Bulletin*

public-health

This list provides a discussion forum and information resource for those working in epidemiology and public health. It aims to facilitate information sharing (e.g. workshops, seminars, conferences and new research) and promote links, collaborative working, joint problem-solving and mutual support. *Type of resource : Discussion list*

To join this list send the command:

join public-health firstname lastname

as the only text of an e-mail message to:

mailbase@mailbase.ac.uk

Public Health Effectiveness Project

Based at McMaster University this project makes available a selection of full-text systematic overviews together with a series of topic files containing high-quality studies in a wide variety of public health topics. *Address:*- Quality of Nursing Worklife Reserach Unit, Faculty of Health Sciences, 2J Reception. 1200 Main Street West, HAMILTON, Ontario, L8N 3Z5. *Type of resource:- Project, WWW site*

http://hiru.hirunet.mcmaster.ca/cgi/hirexs.exe?FOLDER=0@pheffect

Details of the project are found at:-

http://hiru.mcmaster.ca/ohcen/groups/hthu/default.htm

Research & Development (R&D) Strategy pages

Most of these pages deal with the mechanics of the strategy but many practitioners will be interested in research *per se* and will want to keep up to date with the NHS strategy. There are now several home pages. They include a **Department of Health R&D Strategy Home Page.** *Type of resource:- WWW site*

http://www.open.gov.uk/doh/rdd1.htm

All the Regional Offices have committed to having a Regional home page. So far there are five:-

Anglia and Oxford

http://wwwlib.jr2.ox.ac.uk/a-ordd/index.htm

North Thames

http://www.nthames-health.tpmde.ac.uk/ntr/rd.htm

South and West

http://www.epi.bris.ac.uk/rd

Trent

http://www.netlink.co.uk/users/nhstrent/trentrd/rd.html

West Midlands

http://www.gold.net/users/ei26/index.htm

RAND Corporation

RAND is a US-based nonprofit institution that aims to improve public policy through research and analysis. RAND aims to carry out high-quality, objective research addressing problems of domestic policy including health care. RAND has been studying health care issues for more than thirty years. Today, RAND conducts one of the largest private, nonprofit programs of health policy research and analysis in the world. They publish numerous reports and other documents in areas of health care technology assessment. The full-text of some of these is available via their World Wide Web pages. *Type of Resource:- WWW site*

http://www.rand.org/

RevMan

This database is freely available by ftp from the cochrane.co.uk site. It is used for managing the process of a systematic review and is accompanied by a comprehensive manual. (Other software packages are MODMAN and PARENT - see *Cochrane Collaboration Newsletter* Issue 1 August 1994). *Type of Resource:- Software.*

School of Health And Related Research (ScHARR)

This health services research department within the University of Sheffield is involved in finding the evidence (expertise in literature searching); appraising the evidence (critical appraisal training) and producing the evidence (systematic reviews). The Information Resources Section of ScHARR produces a bibliography and resource guide entitled *"The ScHARR Guide to Evidence Based Practice".* Copies are available for £10.00 (inclusive of Postage & Packing) from ScHARR Information Resources at the address below. [Cheques payable to the University of Sheffield]. *Address:-* University of Sheffield, Regent Court, 30 Regent Street, SHEFFIELD, S1 4DA. *Type of resource : Organisation, Information Service, Training Course Provider, WWW resource list, WWW site*

http://www.shef.ac.uk/uni/academic/R-Z/scharr/index.html

ScHARR-Lock's Guide to the Evidence

This is a guide to printed sources of evidence arranged by Medical Subject Heading (MeSH). It focuses on grey literature from UK academic and quasi-governmental sources and aims to complement Michael Zack's list of Evidence-based Topics (See above). Type of resource : *WWW resource list*

http://www.shef.ac.uk/uni/academic/R-Z/scharr/ir/scebm.html

Screening and Diagnostic Tests (Cochrane Collaboration)

The Cochrane Collaboration Methods Working Group on Screening and Diagnostic Tests has placed its recommendations on how to search for, appraise and pool results of studies of diagnostic accuracy on the Web. The document includes a methodological bibliography. *Type of Resource : WWW site.*

http://wwwsom.fmc.flinders.edu.au/COCHRANE/cochrane/sadtdoc1.htm

System for Information on Grey Literature in Europe (SIGLE)

The System for Information on Grey Literature in Europe file is a bibliographic database covering European nonconventional (called grey) literature in the fields of pure and applied sciences and technology. Since 1984, economics, social sciences and humanities also are covered. *SIGLE* provides access to grey literature such as research reports, discussion and policy documents, working and conference papers, theses, some official publications, publications provided by local authorities or industry and others. (Available via *BLAISE*, British Library, Boston Spa, West Yorkshire and via Silverplatter). *Type of Resource: CD-ROM Database, Online Database*

South and West R&D Briefing Papers

The Briefing Papers Series commissioned by the R&D directorate offers brief but authorative discussions on the effectiveness of health interventions. *Type of Resource : WWW site*

http://cochrane.epi.bris.ac.uk/rd/publicat/briefing/index.htm

Swedish Council on Technology Assessment in Health Care (SBU)

SBU's task is to evaluate methods used within health care and to look critically at their costs, their risks and their benefits. SBU assesses the medical, ethical, social and economic impact of new and established medical procedures. *Type of resource : Organisation, WWW presence*

http://www.sbu.se/home.html

Systematic Literature Reviewing

This site at the University of Leeds aims to provide basic information about conducting systematic literature reviews, drawing on the publications of the NHS Centre for Reviews and Dissemination and the Cochrane Collaboration. Although the site is particularly focused on aspects specific to medical imaging the materials provided are generic and include a useful interactive quiz to test basic knowledge of the systematic review process. *Type of resource:- WWW site Computer Assisted Learning*

http://agora.leeds.ac.uk/comir/people/eberry/sysrev/sysrev.htm

Systematic Reviews Training Unit (SRTU)

The Systematic Reviews Training Unit (SRTU), funded for three years from North and South Thames Regional Research and Development Programmes, is a joint initiative of the Institute of Child Health, the Royal Free Hospital School of Medicine and University College London. The Unit is supported by a Collaborative Reviews Group, whose members are drawn from a variety of disciplines including child health, care of the elderly, cardiovascular disease, primary care, genito-urinary medicine and public health medicine. Staff of the Unit work closely with members of the Collaborative Reviews Group, providing training and developing systematic review methodology. The main aims of the Unit are to train health professionals in the conduct of systematic reviews to enable trainees to:

- develop the skills required to formulate answerable questions about the effectiveness of health care practice and policy and conduct systematic reviews of research evidence to address these questions;
- acquire an understanding of methods for effective dissemination and promotion of the implementation of review findings.

Type of resource : Organisation, Training Course Provider, WWW presence

http://www.ich.bpmf.ac.uk/ebm/srtu.htm

Teaching Critical Appraisal Skills (Educational Clearing House)

This resource lists publications, journal articles and privately produced material to assist in the teaching of critical appraisal. *Type of resource:-WWW presence*

http://ww.pitt.edu/~leff/apdim/ch/critapp.htm

Trent Institute for Health Services Research (TIHSR)

The Trent Institute for Health Services Research is a collaborative venture between the Universities of Leicester, Nottingham and Sheffield with support from NHS Executive Trent. The Institute provides advice and support on research, consultancy, training and educational support as well as disseminating the results of research to influence the provision of health care. *Address:-* Trent Institute for Health Services Research (Core Unit), Regent Court, 30 Regent Court, Sheffield S1 4DA. Tel : 0114 222 5446.

Type of resource : Organisation, Training Course Provider, WWW presence

http://www.shef.ac.uk/~scharr/tihsr/tihsr.html

Trent Working Group on Acute Purchasing

ScHARR (see above), which houses the Sheffield Unit of the Trent Institute for Health Services Research, facilitates a Trent Working Group on Acute Purchasing. A list of interventions for consideration is recommended by the purchasing authorities in Trent and approved by the Purchasing Authorities Chief Executives and the Trent Development and Evaluation Committee. After literature searching, health economics and operational research input a seminar, led by a public health consultant, is convened for consideration of the research evidence. The guidance emanating from the seminars is reflected in a series of Guidance Notes. Topics covered to date include:- Tertiary Cardiology, DNase in Cystic Fibrosis, Beta Interferon in Multiple Sclerosis and Cochlear Implants.

Type of resource:- Project

ProSPECT-or Newsletter

This irregular bulletin alerts purchasers to recent items of evidence in topic areas chosen by the Working Group on Acute Purchasing. Available from the Information Resources Section at ScHARR, Regent Court, 30 Regent Street, SHEFFIELD S1 4DA.

Type of resource:- Newsletter

UK Clearing House on Health Outcomes

The UK Clearing House on Health Outcomes was established in the Autumn of 1992. It is based within the Nuffield Institute for Health, at the University of Leeds. The Clearing House aims : to develop and promote approaches to health outcomes assessment within routine health care practice; to encourage a shift from process to outcome measures and the use of patient centred and clinically relevant outcomes criteria; to support the use of process information and existing data sources where it is not yet feasible to measure outcomes directly; to raise awareness about key issues in health outcome measurement; to promote the role of health outcomes within decision making in health care commissioning and provision.

Type of resource:- Type of resource:- Project; Newsletter; Information Service, WWW database. The home page is:-

http://www.leeds.ac.uk/nuffield/infoservices/UKCH/home.html

They have two databases available on the WWW;

Outcomes Activities Database

This contains a wide range of outcomes related projects and forms the basis for networking people working in similar areas or using similar measures:-

http://www.leeds.ac.uk/nuffield/infoservices/UKCH/oad.html/

Outcomes Database Of Structured Abstracts

This provides information on the literature covering the development of outcome measures and the measurement of outcomes in various topic areas:-

http://www.leeds.ac.uk/nuffield/infoservices/UKCH/osad.html/

The Clearing House also produces a newsletter available on subscription:-

Outcomes Briefing

Outcomes Briefing is a bi-annual publication - it covers a range of general issues relating to the measurement of outcomes. Each issue follows a general theme, with additional conference/workshop reports, invited contributions and current awareness literature.

Address:- UK Clearing House on Health Outcomes, Nuffield Institute for Health, University of Leeds, 71-75 Clarendon Road, LEEDS, LS2 9PL.

http://www.leeds.ac.uk/nuffield/infoservices/UKCH/publi.html

UK Primary Care - Evidence Based Medicine

Brief site aimed at the commissioning practice, complete with definitions and links to other UK resources. *Type of resource : WWW presence.* Found at:-

http://www.compulink.co.uk/~hold/ebm.htm

UK Workshops on Teaching Evidence-Based Practice

A number of organisations run workshops on Teaching Evidence Based Practice. To date there have been UK Workshops in Oxford (1st, 1995), London (2nd, 1996), Oxford (3rd, 1996), London (4th, 1997) with a fifth planned for Oxford in June 1997. Other courses have been organised in Evidence Based Child Health (1996 & 1997) and Evidence Based Psychiatry (April 1997). The Centre for Evidence Based Medicine site and the evidence-based-health discussion list are good sources for details of forthcoming courses.

Users' Guides to the Health Care Literature

The Evidence Based Medicine Working Group, a group of clinicians at McMaster and colleagues across North America, have created a set of guides, published in the Journal of the American Medical Association (JAMA). The Users' Guide series aim to assist clinicians to keep up to date in their clinical discipline and to find the best way to manage a particular clinical problem. The User's Guides put much emphasis on integrative studies, including systematic overviews, practice guidelines, decision analysis, and economic analysis. They introduce strategies for efficiently searching the medical literature. *Type of resources:- WWW site.* Full-text of the Guides is available at:-

http://hiru.hirunet.mcmaster.ca/ebm/userguid/default.htm

A comprehensive alphabetical bibliography of references used in the compilation of the User's Guides to the Medical Literature can be found at:

http://hiru.mcmaster.ca/ebm/userguid/ref.htm

A complete list of the published guides, together with their full bibliographic references is available at:-

http://cochrane.epi.bris.ac.uk/rd/links/schebm.htm

Users' Maps for.......

These pages list, for different sources of evidence, the main questions that should be used in critically appraising articles. *Type of resource:- WWW site.* Examples include:-

an Overview

http://hiru.hirunet.mcmaster.ca/ebm/userguid/6_map.htm

a Decision Analysis

http://hiru.hirunet.mcmaster.ca/ebm/userguid/7_map.htm

a Clinical Practice Guideline

http://hiru.hirunet.mcmaster.ca/ebm/userguid/8_map.htm

Warren Magnussen Grant Clinical Center (National Institutes of Health)

Amongst a host of information, this NIH centre has a list of current clinical research studies. There are over 1000 ongoing clinical trials listed and they show the study title, a summary, the sponsoring institute and the patient characteristics needed for enrollment. *Type of resource : WWW database*

http://www.cc.nih.gov/

Welsh Health Gain Investment Protocol Enhancement Project

This project, commissioned by the Welsh Office, aims to enhance twelve policy documents (Protocols for Investment in Health Gain) originally produced by the Welsh Health Planning Forum in the early 1990s by systematically seeking and appraising the best available evidence in each area. Areas covered by the original documents include:- cancers, cardiovascular diseases, healthy environments, healthy living, injuries, maternal and early child health, mental handicap (learning disabilities), mental health, oral health, pain discomfort and palliative care, physical disability and discomfort and respiratory diseases. *Address:-* Protocol Enhancement Project, Sir Herbert Duthie Library, University of Wales College of Medicine, CARDIFF. *Type of resource:- Project*

Wessex Institute for Health Research and Development

Address:- the activities of the Institute are located at three sites : Dawn House, Sleepers Hill, Winchester (Health Technology Assessment); Highcroft, Romsey Road, Winchester (Health Promotion); South Academic Block, Southampton General Hospital (Nutrition, Primary Care, Public Health Research) *Type of resource:- Organisation; Information Service; Software*
http://www.soton.ac.uk/~wi/

Workshops on How to Teach Evidence Based Medicine

McMaster University Department of Clinical Epidemiology and Biostatistics have assembled sets of readings dealing with evidence-based medicine and critical appraisal issues in therapy, diagnosis, prognosis, harm, overviews and economic analysis. Some materials, complete with checklists and cribsheets are available on the Internet, and may be downloaded to support Critical Appraisal skills programmes locally. *Type of resource:- WWW site; Training Course Provider; Training materials*
http://hiru.hirunet.mcmaster.ca/ebm/workshop/

****

If you have any suggestions for inclusion in future editions of this guide or any other amendments please send them to:-

Andrew Booth

Director of Information Resources

ScHARR (**Sc**hool of **H**ealth **A**nd **R**elated **R**esearch)

University of Sheffield

Regent Court

30 Regent Street

SHEFFIELD

S1 4DA

(Tel : +44 (0)114 222 5420)

(Fax : +44 (0) 114 272 4095)

(E-mail : A.Booth@sheffield.ac.uk)

Other papers published in this series by the School of Health and Related Research are listed below:-

No.1   Catching the Tide : New Voyages in Nursing? (1995) by S Read.   £10.00

96/1   A Review of Public Attitudes towards Mental Health Facilities in the   £10.00
       Community (1996) by J Repper and C Brooker.

96/2   An Economic Evaluation of Nabumetone/Relifex compared with   £10.00
       Ibuprofen and a Weighted NSAID Combination (1996) by RL
       Akehurst, M Backhouse, P Emery, I Haslock, J Kirsch, CJ
       McCabe, DL Scott, M Whitfield and AD Woolf.

97/1   Clinical Placements for Student Nurses and Midwives : An   £10.00
       Evaluation of Costs and Practices (1997) by M Lloyd-Jones and
       RL Akehurst

Copies of these documents are available from:-

Suzy Paisley
Senior Information Officer
School of Health Related Research
Regent Court
30 Regent Street
SHEFFIELD S1 4DA

Tel   0114 222 5420
Fax   0114 272 4095
E-mail scharrlib@sheffield.ac.uk

Please make cheques payable to "The University of Sheffield"